Write from Medieval History
Level 1

A Charlotte Mason Writing Program
"Gentle and Complete"

Medieval History
600 AD – 1600 AD

From Caedmon the Poet to Shakespeare

Manuscript Models

Historical Narratives, English Tales, Poetry, and Cultural Tales

© Copyright 2009. Kimberly Garcia. All rights reserved. For permission to make copies of any kind, written or otherwise, please contact the author at www.writefromhistory.com.

Acknowledgements

A huge thank you to my children and husband for their patience.

Table of Contents

Introduction	vi
Definitions—Narration, Copywork, Studied Dictation	viii
Scheduling Information	xi

Chapter I — Historical Narratives

The Cowherd Who Became a Poet, Caedmon	658 – 680	I-3
The Caliph and the Poet	712 – 755	I-10
A Lesson in Humility, Haroun-al-Raschid	786 – 809	I-15
The Sons of the Caliph	786 – 833	I-19
How a Prince Learned to Read, Alfred the Great	871 – 899	I-23
King Alfred and the Cakes, Alfred the Great	849 – 899	I-28
King Alfred and the Beggar	849 – 899	I-33
King Canute on the Seashore	995 – 1035	I-38
The Sons of William the Conqueror	1027 – 1087	I-43
The White Ship, King Henry	1068 – 1135	I-49
The King and His Hawk, Genghis Khan	1162 – 1227	I-55
King John and the Abbot	1166 – 1216	I-61
The Shepherd Boy Painter, Giotto	1267 – 1337	I-68
The Hunted King, Robert I king of the Scots	1274 – 1329	I-73
The Black Douglas	1286 – 1330	I-78
The Story of William Tell	1307	I-83
"TRY, TRY AGAIN!" Tamerlane	1336 – 1405	I-88
Arnold Winkelried	1386	I-93
The Horseshoe Nails, King Richard	1452 – 1485	I-98
King Edward and his Bible	1537 – 1553	I-103
Sir Humphrey Gilbert	1539 – 1583	I-108
Sir Walter Raleigh	1552 – 1618	I-112
Which Was the King? King Henry the Fourth of France	1553 - 1610	I-118
Sir Philip Sidney	1554 – 1586	I-122

Chapter II — English Tales

How Jack Went to Seek His Fortune	II-3
Jack Hannaford	II-9
Lazy Jack	II-15
Little Red Riding Hood	II-20
The Magpie's Nest	II-26
The Miller's Guest	II-31
The Old Woman and Her Pig	II-37
Other Wise Men of Gotham	II-42
Saddle to Rags	II-48
The Shoemaker and the Elves	II-54
A Story of Robin Hood	II-59
The Story of the Three Little Pigs	II-65
Three Men of Gotham	II-71
Tom Thumb	II-76

Chapter III — Poetry from/about Medieval History

Aladdin		III-3
Baa, Baa, Black Sheep		III-6
Cock-A-Doodle-Doo		III-9
Columbus	1451 – 1506	III-12
Rex Arthurus	c. 6th Century	III-15
The Greenwood Tree, Shakespeare	1564-1616	III-18
Ingratitude, Shakespeare	1564-1616	III-21
I Saw a Ship A-Sailing		III-24
Saint Bernard's Hymn	1091 – 1153	III-27
The Sermon of St. Francis	1182 – 1226	III-30
To Market To Market		III-33

Chapter IV[+] — Cultural Tales

The Frog's Travels	Tale from Japan	IV-3
How Indian Corn Came into the World	Ojibbeway Legend	IV-8
The Necklace of Truth	Tale about Merlin	IV-14
The Pancake	Norwegian Tale	IV-20
Tale of a Dumb Witness	Arabian Tale	IV-27
The Three Billy Goats Gruff	Norwegian Tale	IV-32
Why the Bear's Tail Is Short	German Tale	IV-37
The Wolf and the Seven Young Kids	German Tale	IV-42

Appendix

Narration Questions	2
Grammar Guide	3
Models from Chapter I historical narratives	9
Models from Chapter II English Tales	15
Models from Chapter III poetry from or about Medieval history	19
Models from Chapter IV folktales of various cultures	23

+Note: The publication dates for Chapter IV are not included. These are very old tales with many variations published at various times.

Introduction

Write from Medieval History Layout

Write from Medieval History is a writing program that teaches grammar, spelling, penmanship, and history—all at once. This volume covers medieval history from 600 AD to 1600 AD, for the beginning writer.

Write from Medieval History teaches writing the Charlotte Mason way for grades first through third. It is divided into four chapters: short stories, English tales, poetry, and cultural tales. For Chapter I, short stories that give insight into people, places, and events during medieval times have been selected. Chapter II contains tales of English origin that are thought to have been around during the Middle Ages. Chapter III contains poetry from and about medieval times. Chapter IV contains folk tales from various cultures.

In all four chapters, the reading selection is followed by two passages which serve as writing models for the student. The first model has lines immediately below each word and the second model has lines further down the paper. There are more than 55 selections included in *Write from Medieval History*.

To coordinate *Write from Medieval History* with your history topics, refer to the Table of Contents, which also serves as a timeline. Use the timeline provided to determine which selection would be the best fit for that week's history lesson. *Write from Medieval History* can be used with any history program.

All of the works included were taken from the public domain; many have been edited for Write from Medieval History.

Note: Although titles of books and ships would normally be italicized in texts, they are underlined to teach children that these names are underlined in handwritten works.

Most of the principles in *Write from Medieval History* are based on the work of Ms. Charlotte Mason. She advocated that children of the grammar or elementary stage practice narration, copywork, and dictation as their primary method of learning to write. But because Ms. Mason's methods have been interpreted differently over the years, I have included alternatives suggestions on how to implement *Write from Medieval History*. So to begin using *Write from Medieval History* as your child's writing program, please read the entire introduction, pages vi–xi, before your student begins.

Additional Information

Reading Levels
Chapters I and II contain chapters taken from living books that are historically relevant to medieval times. These selections may be above the reading ability of some first and second graders. Chapter III contains poetry that will be above the reading level of many first, second, and third graders. If necessary, read the poetry selections to your student. If you would like to stretch your student, ask him to read the selections back to you. These reading selections offer great opportunity to cover new vocabulary as well as new ideas.

Appendix "Models Only"
The Appendix lists all of the models by chapter. See page x of the Introduction for information on scheduling. To assist the instructor, the Appendix can be removed for the purpose of dictating to the older student.

Getting Started
On the following page, I have covered each area of the program: Narration, Copywork, and Dictation. I have also provided a guide suggesting how to incorporate grammar into the program. Please read these in their entirety.

Correcting Work
Correcting writing can be difficult. Ms. Mason advised teachers and parents to correct the student's writings occasionally. This makes perfect sense when realizing that Ms. Mason's methods did not require the need for extensive corrections. She consistently emphasized that work be done correctly the first time. This takes more effort on the part of the teacher when the student is a beginning writer. For the beginning writer, the teacher should be present during copywork to ensure that the student is forming letters correctly. During dictation, Ms. Mason believed that student should not be allowed to visually dwell on incorrect work. When a child made a mistake, she had stamps or pieces of paper available to cover the mistakes so that they were not visually reinforced.

When a child made a mistake during narrations, Ms. Mason withheld correcting him. I believe that she used the time after the narration was finished to discuss the material that had been narrated.

When corrections are needed, it is good to practice the principle of praise before correcting children. Find out what is right with what they've done. Be impressed. Focus on their effort. Build them up. In Ephesians 5:29 of the King James Bible, it says—

Let no corrupt communication
proceed out of your mouth, but
that which is good to the use of edifying,
that it may minister grace
unto the hearers.

The hearers are our students—our children. And the words we say will either minister grace or condemnation. We must encourage them and free them from the fear of our frustrations and negative feedback as we correct them.

Definitions
Personal Narrations – the act of retelling

Ms. Mason believed narrations should be done immediately after the story was read to the student or by the student. Narrations are very simple, yet very effective in teaching writing. Narrating helps children to internalize the content of the reading material they have been exposed to and allows them to make it their own. In order to narrate, students must listen carefully, dissect the information, and then express that same information in their own words. It is a powerful tool, but very simple to put into practice.

Oral narrations **Read all or part of the story only once before requiring the student to narrate! It will require him to pay attention.** Simply ask your student to tell you what he has just heard or read.

If your student has trouble with this process, show him how to narrate by demonstrating the process for him. **Read a selection yourself and then narrate it to him. Ask him to imitate you.** If he continues to draw a blank, use the list of questions below to prompt him.

Besides all of the previously mentioned benefits, oral narrations teach students to digest information, dissect it, and reorganize it into their own words while thinking on their feet. This practice helps students to develop the art of public speaking. This formal process will force them to express their ideas without a written plan. It strengthens the mind. And over time, their speech will become fluent and natural. (I sometimes have my children stand as they narrate. It makes the process more formal.)

If your student has difficulty with narrations, ask some or all of the following questions:

1. Who was the main character?
2. What was the character like?
3. Where was the character?
4. What time was it in the story?
5. Who else was in the story?
6. Does the main character have an enemy?
   (The enemy may be another character, himself, or nature.)
7. Did the main character have a problem? If not, what did the character want?
8. What does the main character do? What does he say? If there are others, what do they do?
9. Why does the character do what he does?
10. What happens to the character as he tries to solve his problem?
11. Is there a moral to the story? If so, what was it?
12. What happens at the end of the story? Or how does the main character finally solve his problem?

Written Summations
Most first and second graders will not be ready to write their own summations. Until they are, students dictate and parents write. Written Summations are different from oral narrations. The oral narrations allow the students to demonstrate all that they have learned from the reading selection. Summaries, however, focus on the most important aspects of the selection—the beginning, the middle, and the end as well as the who, what, when, where, why, and how.

Around the age of 10, Ms. Mason required students to write down their narrations, for themselves. Many students can do this earlier. Written summations will allow your student to develop this skill. If your student is able, have him write as much as he can, as perfectly as he can, even around the age of 8.

At the end of each oral narration, ask your child to summarize the reading selection by identifying the beginning, the middle, and the end. He should be able to do this in about three to six sentences. Younger students will sometimes begin each sentence with "First,..." or "At the beginning,..." This is okay. But once the student masters the summation, ask him to summarize without these types of words. Tell him to begin with the subject or the time.

> Ex: When Louisa May Alcott was a young girl, she was very happy because she spent her time playing with her sisters and writing in her diary.

The benefits of written summations are manifold. They will help your student to think linearly from the beginning of the reading selection to the end. They also provide the right amount of content for the beginning writer. When you feel that your student is ready, help him to write the first sentence of his summation, allow him to dictate the remaining sentences to you.

Additionally, the act of summarizing teaches students to identify the main thread or central idea of a passage. Even though your child begins to write his written summations, have him continue his oral narrations without limit. These will help him to internalize and learn the historical content of the stories in *Write from Medieval History* as well develop his public speaking skills.

Copywork and Grammar—copying a passage exactly as written

As your child copies the model before him, stay near so that you are able to correct any problems immediately. Ms. Mason was a strong advocate in learning a skill correctly the first time.

Before your child begins, discuss the model with him. Point out the grammatical elements that he is learning. Have your child copy the model. If you are studying grammar via the models, have him identify a part of speech in the model and circle it with a colored pencil. See page 3 of the Appendix for a grammar guide. (Spend as long as necessary on each part of speech. This means that some first graders may only cover nouns, verbs, and pronouns during one school year. This is definitely okay!) When using the grammar guide, continue to review by including all previously learned work in the current lesson. Once nouns are learned, the student is to identify both nouns and verbs. Thereafter—nouns, verbs, and pronouns.

Ms. Mason recommended the formal study of grammar at about 4th or 5th grade. If you opt to add a formal program for your beginning writer, that would be fine. If you do so, feel free to omit the grammar study in this program.

The grammar guide contains more grammar than is necessary for first and second graders. At this level, students only focus on learning the parts of speech and the punctuation necessary to correctly write the four types of sentences.

Studied Dictation—the act of writing from an oral reading

(Many students will not be ready for dictation at this level. If you child masters copywork, feel free to introduce dictation.)

Once again, Ms. Mason's ideas are simple, yet effective. The goal in dictation is to teach your child to write correctly, and from memory, the sentences or clauses he has just heard. Ms. Mason let the child study the dictation model for a few minutes. She wrote down any unknown words on a board that were more difficult for him. She then erased the board and read each passage only once. From this one reading, the child wrote; however, if the child made a mistake, Ms. Mason covered the mistake instantly so that the student was not allowed to visualize and internalize it.

If you would like to introduce your second or third grader to dictation, feel free to reduce the model to an appropriate length for your student. For the child who has never done dictation, this may be a sentence of only a few words. Read the passage as many times as necessary. Work down to one reading per sentence. This is an advanced skill and may require time to achieve. Be patient, but consistent. (If needed, allow your student to repeat the model back to you before he writes. Some students may need this reinforcement; others may not.)

After you write the dictation model on the whiteboard, discuss it, in depth, with your student. An example of the process follows.

MODEL

The bolded paragraphs below are the model for this exercise.

"Did Mary spill the ink on the carpet?" asked Tom.
"No," answered Mary. "Did you, Will?"
"I did not, Mary, but I know who did," said Will.
"Who was it, Will?"
Will did not answer in words. He pointed a finger at Fido, and guilty little Fido crept under the sofa.

For the student that is new to dictation, determine the size of the model. In the dialogue above, the bolded words represent the sentences that are to be discussed for studied dictation.

Because the student is new to dictation, do not expect him to understand the grammar if he has not been taught it before. So first, determine which grammatical elements you will be teaching. For this example, we are focusing on proper and common nouns, as well as questions and statements.

QUESTIONS TO ASK:

1. What are the names of the people in this story? How does each name begin?
2. Do you remember what a noun is? A noun is the word that names a person, place, thing, or idea. Can you find any nouns in the first paragraph?
3. Do you see that some nouns are not capitalized and some are?
4. Common nouns are not capitalized. Common nouns name any item of a group—like any boy, girl, or building. However, proper nouns name specific boys, girls, or buildings—Jimmy Brown, Mary Black, or Tom Swift.
5. Do you remember what a question is? Can you find a question mark in the first sentence?
6. Can you make up some questions of your own?
    Sentences that end in question marks are called questions or interrogative sentences.
7. Sentences that end in periods are called declarative sentences or statements. Can you find a period in the first sentence or the second?

If there are any questions that your student cannot answer, tell him the answers. Discuss the grammar with him, and work with him until he can narrate why the model is punctuated the way it is.

Do the same with spelling. Identify the words that your student doesn't know and discuss why those words are spelled the way they are.

Scheduling Information

Listed below is a recommendation for the use of *Write from Medieval History*; however, this is **only a recommendation** and should be adjusted for your student's individual needs. **Further explanations and alternate methods** are included on the next page. Please feel free to adjust these methods to make writing as painless as possible for your student. Every child is different.

One Suggested Schedule:

Day 1 **Reading, Oral Narration, and Written Summation**
From the Table of Contents, choose a story.
Either you or your student should read the story selection once.
First, have the student orally narrate to you.
If he has difficulty, demonstrate how to narrate and then ask him to imitate you.
If he still cannot narrate the story, use the narration questions listed in the Appendix. (Optional: ask your student to summarize the story in about three sentences to six sentences. If he is able, have him write one or more sentences from his summation.) Write for him, if needed.
(For more on narrations, see page viii.)

Day 2 **Copywork and Grammar** Complete Model Practice 1 from Day 1's reading selection. Discuss/explain the grammar and punctuation in the model.
Do a color-coded grammar study.
(For more on copywork and grammar, see page ix.)
(See page 3 and 4 of the Appendix for the grammar guide)

Day 3 **Copywork and Grammar** Complete Model Practice 2, also from Day 1's reading selection. Discuss/explain the grammar and punctuation in the model.
Do a color-coded grammar study.
(See page 3 and 4 of the Appendix for the grammar guide)

Day 4 **Reading, Oral narration, and Copywork**
From the Table of Contents, choose a story or poem.
He may read the poem himself. If so, teach him to read with expression.
Have your student orally narrate what he has learned. Use Model Practice 1 for copywork. Discuss/explain the grammar and punctuation in the model.
Do a color-coded grammar study.
(See page 3 and 4 of the Appendix for the grammar guide)

Day 5 **Copywork and Grammar** Complete Model Practice 2, also from Day 4's reading selection. Discuss/explain the grammar and punctuation in the model.
Do a color-coded grammar study.
(See page 3 and 4 of the Appendix for the grammar guide)

If the models are too long

If the models are too long for your student, reduce them. Beginning writers should not be forced to do more than they are able.

If your child is ready for dictation

Use either the first or second model as dictation. The Appendix contains a list of all models used in *Write from Medieval History*. Remove and use to dictate to your student.

Optional Schedules

Charlotte Mason's Methods

Ms. Mason used narration, copywork, and dictation simultaneously throughout a young child's education. Narrations were done immediately after they had listened to or read the selection. Copywork was done from well-written sentences. And although many don't believe copywork to be valuable once a student learns to write from dictation, Ms. Mason believed that copywork was extremely valuable for many years alongside dictation. Dictation was a separate part of the process, mostly for the purpose of teaching spelling.

Ms. Mason allowed students to look at the dictation passages and study them before the student began writing. This process was helpful because it allowed the student to visualize how the passage should look. It taught him to study with intent and to focus on each individual word. After the passage was read once, the student wrote the passage from memory. This method improved a child's spelling and his grasp of correct punctuation, as well.

But not everyone who follows Ms. Mason's methods follows each area of narration, copywork, and dictation in the same way. Below are some ways to incorporate some or all of these ideas into your child's learning adventure.

Different Copywork Passages Daily

If followed, the schedule on the previous page will provide your student with four separate copywork passages per week.

Copywork as Dictation

If you would like to introduce your child to dictation by using the same model, you may use the first model provided as copywork and dictation. Have your student copy the passage on day 2 and write it from dictation on day 3. He should write the dictation work in the model practice 3 area.

Copywork and Dictation

If you would like to use the second model for dictation rather than copywork, cover the passage in the text and dictate the model to your student. You may use the student's model, which is provided in the student's book, for studied dictation. With studied dictation, the student studies the model for unknown words and works on memorizing them. When he is ready, cover the model with a slip of sticky paper and dictate while he writes. The Appendix contains a list of all models for the instructor's use.

More on Studied Dictation

Once again, Ms. Mason's ideas are simple, yet effective. The goal in dictation is to teach your child to write correctly and from memory the sentences or clauses he has just heard. Ms. Mason let the child study the dictation for a few minutes. She wrote on a board any unknown words that were more difficult for him. She then erased the board and read each passage only once. From this one reading, the child wrote; however, if the child made a mistake, she covered the mistake instantly so that the student was not allowed to visualize and internalize the mistake.

For the child who has never done dictation, start by reading as many times as necessary so that your child memorizes the sentences. ***Work down to one reading per model***. This is an advanced skill and may require time to achieve. Be patient, but consistent. (If needed, allow your student to repeat the model back to you before he writes. Some students may need this reinforcement; others may not.)

Reminders and Helps

- Use *Write from Medieval History* in the best way possible to serve your student's needs. Adapt any area, as necessary.
- Help students with spelling, as necessary. Set your student up for success.
- In the case of dialogue, remind your student that each time a different character is speaking, a new paragraph is started via indentions. When they first encounter this, show them an example before requiring them to do this.
- If the size of the selection is too large, **simply reduce it and require less.**
- Set your student up for success. He shouldn't be expected to know what he has not yet been taught.
- To sum up Charlotte Mason's methods:

Quality over quantity.
Accuracy over speed.
Ideas over drill.
Perfection over mediocrity.

CHAPTER I

Historical Narratives from Medieval Times

(Models taken from the beginning of a paragraph in the original selection are indented.)

The Cowherd Who Became a Poet, Caedmon

(658-680)
from Fifty Famous People
by James Baldwin

In England there was once a famous abbey, called Whitby. It was so close to the sea that those who lived in it could hear the waves forever beating against the shore. The land around it was rugged, with only a few fields in the midst of a vast forest.

In those far-off days, an abbey was half church, half castle. It was a place where good people and timid, helpless people could find shelter in time of war. There they might live in peace and safety, while all the country round was overrun by rude and barbarous men.

One cold night in winter, the serving men of the abbey were gathered in the great kitchen. They were sitting around the fire and trying to keep themselves warm.

Out of doors the wind was blowing. The men heard it as it whistled through the trees and rattled the doors of the abbey. They drew up closer to the fire and felt thankful that they were safe from the raging storm. "Who will sing us a song?" said the master woodman as he threw a fresh log upon the fire.

"Yes, a song! A song!" shouted some of the others. "Let us have a good old song that will help to keep us warm."

"We can all be minstrels tonight," said the chief cook. "Suppose we each sing a song in turn. What say you?"

"Agreed! Agreed!" cried the others. "And the cook shall begin."

The woodman stirred the fire until the flames leaped high and the sparks flew out of the roof hole. Then the chief cook began his song. He sang of war, and of bold rough deeds, and of love and sorrow.

After him, the other men were called, one by one; and each in turn sang his favorite song. The woodman sang of the wild forest; the plowman sang of the fields; the shepherd sang of his sheep; and those who listened forgot about the storm and the cold weather.

But in the corner, almost hidden from his fellows, one poor man was sitting who did not enjoy the singing. It was Caedmon, the cowherd. "What shall I do when it comes my turn?" he said to himself.

"I do not know any song. My voice is harsh and I cannot sing."

So he sat there trembling and afraid; for he was a timid, bashful man and did not like to be noticed.

At last, just as the blacksmith was in the midst of a stirring song, he rose quietly and went out into the darkness. He went across the narrow yard to the sheds where the cattle were kept in stormy weather.

"The gentle cows will not ask a song of me," said the poor man. He soon found a warm corner, and there he lay down, covering himself with the straw.

Inside of the great kitchen, beside the fire, the men were shouting and laughing; for the blacksmith had finished his song, and it was very pleasing.

"Who is next?" asked the woodman.

"Caedmon, the keeper of the cows," answered the chief cook.

"Yes, Caedmon! Caedmon!" all shouted together. "A song from Caedmon!" But when they looked, they saw that his seat was vacant.

"The poor, timid fellow!" said the blacksmith. "He was afraid and has slipped away from us."

In his safe, warm place in the straw, Caedmon soon fell asleep. All around him were the cows of the abbey, some chewing their cuds, and others like their master quietly sleeping. The singing in the kitchen was ended, the fire had burned low, and each man had gone to his place.

Then Caedmon had a strange dream. He thought that a wonderful light was shining around him. His eyes were dazzled by it. He rubbed them with his hands, and when they were quite open he thought that he saw a beautiful face looking down upon him, and that a gentle voice said, --

"Caedmon, sing for me."

At first, he was so bewildered that he could not answer. Then he heard the voice again.

"Caedmon, sing something."

"Oh, I cannot sing," answered the poor man." I do not know any song; and my voice is harsh and unpleasant. It was for this reason that I left my fellows in the abbey kitchen and came here to be alone."

"But you _must_ sing," said the voice. "You _must_ sing."

"What shall I sing?" he asked.

"Sing of the creation," was the answer.

Then Caedmon, with only the cows as his hearers, opened his mouth and began to sing. He sang of the beginning of things; how the world was made; how the sun and moon came into being; how the land rose from the water; how the birds and the beasts were given life.

All through the night, he sat among the abbey cows, and sang his wonderful song. When the stable boys and shepherds came out in the morning, they heard him singing; and they were so amazed that they stood still in the drifted snow and listened with open mouths.

At length, others of the servants heard him, and were entranced by his wonderful song. And one ran quickly and told the good abbess, or mistress of the abbey, what strange thing had happened.

"Bring the cowherd hither, that I and those who are with me may hear him," said she.

So Caedmon was led into the great hall of the abbey. And all of the sweet-faced sisters and other women of the place listened while he sang again the wonderful song of the creation.

"Surely," said the abbess, "this is a poem, most sweet, most true, most beautiful. It must be written down so that people in other places and in other times may hear it read and sung."

So she called her clerk, who was a scholar, and bade him write the song, word for word, as it came from Caedmon's lips. And this he did.

Such was the way in which the first true English poem was written. And Caedmon, the poor cowherd of the abbey, was the first great poet of England.

Written Summation

Caedmon did not lik singing so he went to the stables. ~~then~~ then he had a dream and after that he sang the song of creation

---

It was stormy and cold at the abbey, and the workers huddled in the kitchen because they were cold. Then the cook suggested they all sing their favorite song. But caedomon, who was the cow hearder, had a ruff voice and did not know any song. So he slipped out and went to the stables to be alone. There in the hay he fell asleep. Caedemon had a strange dream telling him to sing, to sing the song of creation. Then, the sheepherders and other workers came to the stables and herd his song. They told their mistress and caedemon was summoned to sing the song of creaton. The mistress demanded it be written down word for word.

Model Practice 1 (adapted from the original)

Out of doors the wind was blowing. The men heard it as it whistled through the trees.

Then Caedmon had a strange dream. He thought that a wonderful light was shining around him.

Model Practice 2

Model Practice 3

The Caliph and the Poet

712 - 755
from Fifty Famous People
by James Baldwin

Once upon a time there was a famous Arab whose name was Al Mansur. He was the ruler of all the Arabs, and was therefore called the caliph.

Al Mansur loved poetry and was fond of hearing poets repeat their own verses. Sometimes, if a poem was very pleasing, he gave the poet a prize. One day a poet whose name was Thalibi came to the caliph and recited a long poem. When he had finished, he bowed and waited, hoping that he would be rewarded.

"Which would you rather have" asked the caliph, "three hundred pieces of gold, or three wise sayings from my lips?"

The poet wished very much to please the caliph. So he said, "Oh, my master, everybody should choose wisdom rather than wealth."

The caliph smiled, and said, "Very well, then, listen to my first wise saying: When your coat is worn out, don't sew on a new patch; it will look ugly."

"Oh, dear!" moaned the poet. "There go a hundred gold pieces all at once." The caliph smiled again. Then he said, "Listen now to my second word of wisdom. It is this: When you oil your beard, don't oil it too much, lest it soil your clothing."

"Worse and worse!" groaned the poor poet. "There go the second hundred. What shall I do?"

"Wait, and I will tell you," said the caliph; and he smiled again. "My third wise saying is--"

"O caliph, have mercy!" cried the poet. "Keep the third piece of wisdom for your own use, and let me have the gold."

The caliph laughed outright, and so did every one that heard him. Then he ordered his treasurer to pay the poet five hundred pieces of gold. For, indeed, the poem, which he had recited, was wonderfully fine.

The caliph, Al Mansur, lived nearly twelve hundred years ago. He was the builder of a famous and beautiful city called Bagdad.

Written Summation

Model Practice 1 (adapted from the original)

Al Mansur loved poetry

and was fond of hearing

poets repeat their own

verses. Sometimes, he

gave the poet a prize.

The caliph laughed outright, and so did every one that heard him. Then he ordered his treasurer to pay the poet five hundred pieces of gold.

Model Practice 2

Model Practice 3

A Lesson in Humility, Haroun-al-Raschid
786 - 809
from Fifty Famous People
by James Baldwin

One day the caliph, Haroun-al-Raschid, made a great feast. The feast was held in the grandest room of the palace. The walls and ceiling glittered with gold and precious gems. The table was decorated with rare and beautiful plants and flowers.

All the noblest men of Persia and Arabia were there. Many wise men and poets and musicians had also been invited.

In the midst of the feast, the caliph called upon the poet, Abul Atayah, and said, "O Prince of Verse Makers, show us thy skill. Describe in verse this glad and glorious feast."

The poet rose and began: "Live, O caliph and enjoy thyself in the shelter of thy lofty palace."

"That is a good beginning," said Raschid. "Let us hear the rest." The poet went on: "May each morning bring thee some new joy. May each evening see that all thy wishes have been performed."

"Good! Good!" said the caliph, "Go on."

The poet bowed his head and obeyed: "But when the hour of death comes, O my caliph, then alas! Thou wilt learn that all thy delights were but a shadow."

The caliph's eyes were filled with tears. Emotion choked him. He covered his face and wept.

Then one of the officers, who was sitting near the poet, cried out: "Stop! The caliph wished you to amuse him with pleasant thoughts, and you have filled his mind with melancholy."

"Let the poet alone," said Raschid. "He has seen me in my blindness, and is trying to open my eyes."

Haroun-al-Raschid (Aaron the Just) was the greatest of all the caliphs of Bagdad. In a wonderful book, called "The Arabian Nights," there are many interesting stories about him.

Written Summation

Model Practice 1

All the noblest men of

Persia and Arabia were

there. Many wise men and

poets and musicians had also

been invited.

The caliph's eyes were filled with tears. Emotion choked him. He covered his face and wept.

Model Practice 2

Model Practice 3

The Sons of the Caliph
786 - 833
from Fifty Famous People
by James Baldwin

There was a caliph of Persia whose name was Al Mamoun. He had two sons whom he wished to become honest and noble men. So he employed a wise man whose name was Al Farra to be their teacher. One day, after lesson hours, Al Farra rose to go out of the house. The two boys saw him and ran to fetch his shoes. For in that country, people never wear shoes in the house, but take them off at the door. The two boys ran for the teacher's shoes, and each claimed the honor of carrying them to him. But they dared not quarrel and at last agreed that each should carry one shoe. Thus, the honor would be divided. When the caliph heard of this, he sent for Al Farra and asked him, "Who is the most honored of men?"

The teacher answered, "I know of no man who is more honored than yourself."

"No, no," said the caliph. "It is the man who rose to go out, and two young princes contended for the honor of giving him his shoes, but at last agreed that each should offer him one."

Al Farra answered, "Sir, I should have forbidden them to do this. But I feared to discourage them. I hope that I shall never do anything to make them careless of their duties."

"Well," said the caliph, "if you had forbidden them thus to honor you, I should have declared you in the wrong. They did nothing that was beneath the dignity of princes. Indeed, they honored themselves by honoring you." Al Farra bowed low, but said nothing; and the caliph went on. "No young man nor boy," said he, "can be so high in rank as to neglect three great duties: he must respect his ruler, he must love and obey his father, and he must honor his teacher."

Then he called the two young princes to him. And as a reward for their noble conduct, he filled their pockets with gold.

Written Summation

Model Practice 1

But they dared not

quarrel and at last agreed

that each should carry one

shoe. Thus, the honor

would be divided.

They did nothing that was beneath the dignity of princes. Indeed, they honored themselves by honoring you.

Model Practice 2

Model Practice 3

How a Prince Learned to Read
871 - 899
from Fifty Famous People
by James Baldwin

A thousand years ago, boys and girls did not learn to read. Books were very scarce and very precious, and only a few men could read them.

Each book was written with a pen or a brush. The pictures were painted by hand, and some of them were very beautiful. A good book would sometimes cost as much as a good house.

In those times, there were even some kings who could not read. They thought more of hunting and fighting than of learning.

There was one such king who had four sons, Ethelbald, Ethelbert, Ethelred, and Alfred. The three older boys were sturdy, half-grown lads; the youngest, Alfred, was a slender, fair-haired child.

One day when they were with their mother, she showed them a wonderful book that some rich friend had given her. She turned the leaves and showed them the strange letters. She showed them the beautiful pictures and told them how they had been drawn and painted.

They admired the book very much, for they had never seen anything like it. "But the best part of it is the story which it tells," said their mother. "If you could only read, you might learn that story and enjoy it. Now I have a mind to give this book to one of you"

"Will you give it to me, mother?" asked little Alfred.

"I will give it to the one who first learns to read in it," she answered.

"I am sure I would rather have a good bow with arrows," said Ethelred.

"And I would rather have a young hawk that has been trained to hunt," said Ethelbert.

"If I were a priest or a monk," said Ethelbald, "I would learn to read. But I am a prince, and it is foolish for princes to waste their time with such things."

"But I should like to know the story which this book tells," said Alfred.

A few weeks passed by. Then one morning, Alfred went into his mother's room with a smiling, joyous face.

"Mother," he said, "will you let me see that beautiful book again?"

His mother unlocked her cabinet and took the precious volume from its place of safekeeping.

Alfred opened it with careful fingers. Then he began with the first word on the first page and read the first story aloud without making one mistake.

"O, my child, how did you learn to do that?" cried his mother.

"I asked the monk, Brother Felix, to teach me," said Alfred. "And every day since you showed me the book, he has given me a lesson. It was no easy thing to learn these letters and how they are put together to make words. Now, Brother Felix says I can read almost as well as he."

"How wonderful!" said his mother.

"How foolish!" said Ethelbald.

"You will be a good monk when you grow up," said Ethelred with a sneer.

But his mother kissed him and gave him the beautiful book. "The prize is yours, Alfred," she said. "I am sure that whether you grow up to be a monk or a king, you will be a wise and noble man."

And Alfred did grow up to become the wisest and noblest king that England ever had. In history, he is called Alfred the Great.

Written Summation

Model Practice 1

A thousand years ago, boys and girls did not learn to read. Books were very scarce and very precious.

A few weeks passed by. Then one morning, Alfred went into his mother's room with a smiling, joyous face.

Model Practice 2

Model Practice 3

King Alfred and the Cakes, Alfred the Great
849 - 899
from Fifty Famous Stories Retold
by James Baldwin

Many years ago, there lived in England a wise and good king whose name was Alfred. No other man ever did so much for his country as he; and people now, all over the world, speak of him as Alfred the Great.

In those days, a king did not have a very easy life. There was war almost all the time, and no one else could lead his army into battle so well as he. And so, between ruling and fighting, he had a busy time of it indeed.

A fierce, rude people called the Danes had come from over the sea and were fighting the English. There were so many of them, and they were so bold and strong, that for a long time they gained every battle. If they kept on, they would soon be the masters of the whole country.

At last, after a great battle, the English army was broken up and scattered. Every man had to save himself in the best way he could. King Alfred fled alone, in great haste, through the woods and swamps.

Late in the day, the king came to the hut of a woodcutter. He was very tired and hungry, and he begged the woodcutter's wife to give him something to eat and a place to sleep in her hut.

The woman was baking some cakes upon the hearth, and she looked with pity upon the poor, ragged fellow who seemed so hungry. She had no thought that he was the king.

"Yes," she said, "I will give you some supper if you will watch these cakes. I want to go out and milk the cow, and you must see that they do not burn while I am gone."

King Alfred was very willing to watch the cakes, but he had far greater things to think about. How was he going to get his army together again? And how was he going to drive the fierce Danes out of the land? He forgot his hunger.

He forgot the cakes. He forgot that he was in the woodcutter's hut. His mind was busy making plans for tomorrow.

In a little while, the woman came back. The cakes were smoking on the hearth. They were burned to a crisp. Ah, how angry she was!

"You lazy fellow!" she cried. "See what you have done! You want something to eat, but you do not want to work!"

I have been told that she even struck the king with a stick, but I can hardly believe that she was so ill natured.

The king must have laughed to himself at the thought of being scolded in this way. And he was so hungry that he did not mind the woman's angry words half so much as the loss of the cakes.

I do not know whether he had anything to eat that night, or whether he had to go to bed without his supper. But it was not many days until he had gathered his men together again and had beaten the Danes in a great battle.

Written Summation

Model Practice 1

King Alfred was very

willing to watch the cakes,

but he had far greater

things to think about.

In a little while, the woman came back. The cakes were smoking on the hearth. They were burned to a crisp. Ah, how angry she was!

Model Practice 2

Model Practice 3

King Alfred and the Beggar
from Fifty Famous Stories Retold
by James Baldwin
849 899

At one time, the Danes drove King Alfred from his kingdom, and he had to lie hidden for a long time on a little island in a river.

One day, all who were on the island, except the king and queen and one servant, went out to fish. It was a very lonely place, and no one could get to it except by boat. About noon, a ragged beggar came to the king's door and asked for food.

The king called the servant and asked, "How much food have we in the house?"

"My lord," said the servant, "we have only one loaf and a little wine."

Then the king gave thanks to God, and said, "Give half of the loaf and half of the wine to this poor man."

The servant did as he was bidden. The beggar thanked the king for his kindness and went on his way.

In the afternoon, the men who had gone out to fish came back. They had three boats full of fish, and they said, "We have caught more fish today than in all the other days that we have been on this island."

The king was glad, and he and his people were more hopeful than they had ever been before.

When night came, the king lay awake for a long time and thought about the things that had happened that day. At last, he fancied that he saw a great light like the sun, and in the midst of the light, there stood an old man with black hair, holding an open book in his hand.

It may all have been a dream, and yet to the king it seemed very real indeed. He looked and wondered, but was not afraid.

"Who are you?" he asked of the old man.

"Alfred, my son, be brave," said the man, "for I am the one to whom you gave this day the half of all the food that you had. Be strong and joyful of heart and listen to what I say. Rise up early in the morning and blow your horn three times so loudly that the Danes may hear it. By nine o'clock, five hundred men will be around you ready to be led into battle. Go forth bravely, and within seven days your enemies shall be beaten, and you shall go back to your kingdom to reign in peace."

Then the light went out, and the man was seen no more.

In the morning, the king arose early and crossed over to the mainland. Then he blew his horn three times very loudly. When his friends heard it, they were glad, but the Danes were filled with fear.

At nine o'clock, five hundred of his bravest soldiers stood around him ready for battle. He spoke and told them what he had seen and heard in his dream. When he had finished, they all cheered loudly and said that they would follow him and fight for him so long as they had strength.

So they went out bravely to battle; and they beat the Danes and drove them back into their own place. And King Alfred ruled wisely and well over all his people for the rest of his days.

Written Summation

Model Practice 1

About noon, a ragged

beggar came to the king's

door and asked for

food.

In the morning, the king arose early and crossed over to the main-land. Then he blew his horn three times very loudly.

Model Practice 2

Model Practice 3

King Canute on the Seashore
995 - 1035
from Fifty Famous Stories Retold
by James Baldwin

A hundred years or more after the time of Alfred the Great there was a king of England named Canute. King Canute was a Dane, but the Danes were not so fierce and cruel then as they had been when they were at war with King Alfred.

The great men and officers who were around King Canute were always praising him.

"You are the greatest man that ever lived," one would say.

Then another would say, "O king! There can never be another man so mighty as you."

And another would say, "Great Canute, there is nothing in the world that dares to disobey you."

The king was a man of sense. And he grew very tired of hearing such foolish speeches.

One day he was by the seashore, and his officers were with him. They were praising him, as they were in the habit of doing. He thought that now he would teach them a lesson, and so he bade them set his chair on the beach close by the edge of the water.

"Am I the greatest man in the world?" he asked.

"O king!" they cried, "there is no one so mighty as you."

"Do all things obey me?" he asked.

"There is nothing that dares to disobey you, O king!" they said. "The world bows before you and gives you honor."

"Will the sea obey me?" he asked; and he looked down at the little waves, which were lapping the sand at his feet.

"Sea, I command you to come no farther!"

The foolish officers were puzzled, but they did not dare to say "No."

"Command it, O king, and it will obey!" said one.

"Sea," cried Canute, "I command you to come no farther! Waves, stop your rolling, and do not dare to touch my feet!"

But the tide came in, just as it always did. The water rose higher and higher. It came up around the king's chair and wet not only his feet, but also his robe. His officers stood about him, alarmed, and wondering whether he was not mad.

Then Canute took off his crown and threw it down upon the sand.

"I shall never wear it again," he said. "And you, my men, learn a lesson from what you have seen. There is only one King who is all-powerful, and it is he who rules the sea and holds the ocean in the hollow of his hand. It is he whom you ought to praise and serve above all others."

Written Summation

Model Practice 1

The great men and

officers who were around

King Canute were always

praising him.

The king was a man of sense.
He grew very tired of hearing such
foolish speeches.

Model Practice 2

Model Practice 3

The Sons of William the Conqueror
1027 - 1087
from Fifty Famous Stories Retold
by James Baldwin

There was once a great king of England who was called William the Conqueror. He had three sons.

One day King William seemed to be thinking of something that made him feel very sad, and the wise men who were about him asked him what was the matter.

"I am thinking," he said, "of what my sons may do after I am dead. For, unless they are wise and strong, they cannot keep the kingdom which I have won for them. Indeed, I am at a loss to know which one of the three ought to be the king when I am gone."

"O king!" said the wise men. "If we only knew what things your sons admire the most, we might be able to tell what kind of men they will be. Perhaps, by asking each one of them a few questions, we can find out which one of them will be best fitted to rule in your place."

"The plan is well worth trying, at least," said the king. "Have the boys come before you and then ask them what you please."

The wise men talked with one another for a little while. They agreed that the young princes should be brought in, one at a time, and that the same questions should be put to each.

The first who came into the room was Robert. He was a tall, willful lad and was nicknamed Short Stocking.

"Fair sir," said one of the men, "answer me this question. If, instead of being a boy, it had pleased God that you should be a bird, what kind of a bird would you rather be?"

"A hawk," answered Robert. "I would rather be a hawk, for no other bird reminds one so much of a bold and gallant knight."

The next who came was young William, his father's namesake and pet. His face was jolly and round. And because he had red hair, he was nicknamed Rufus, or the Red.

"Fair sir," said the wise man, "answer me this question. If, instead of being a boy, it had pleased God that you should be a bird, what kind of a bird would you rather be?"

"An eagle," answered William. "I would rather be an eagle, because it is strong and brave. It is feared by all other birds and is therefore the king of them all."

Lastly came the youngest brother, Henry, with quiet steps and a sober, thoughtful look. He had been taught to read and write, and for that reason, he was nicknamed Beau-clerc, or the Handsome Scholar.

"Fair sir," said the wise man, "answer me this question. If, instead of being a boy, it had pleased God that you should be a bird, what kind of a bird would you rather be?"

"A starling," said Henry. "I would rather be a starling, because it is good-mannered and kind and a joy to every one who sees it. And it never tries to rob or abuse its neighbor."

Then the wise men talked with one another for a little while. And when they had agreed among themselves, they spoke to the king.

"We find," said they, "that your eldest son, Robert, will be bold and gallant. He will do some great deeds and make a name for himself. But in the end, he will be overcome by his foes and will die in prison.

"The second son, William, will be as brave and strong as the eagle, but he will be feared and hated for his cruel deeds. He will lead a wicked life and will die a shameful death.

"The youngest son, Henry, will be wise and prudent and peaceful. He will go to war only when he is forced to do so by his enemies. He will be loved at home and respected abroad. And he will die in peace after having gained great possessions."

Years passed by, and the three boys had grown up to be men. King William lay upon his deathbed, and again he thought of what would become of his sons when he was gone. Then he remembered what the wise men had told him. And so he declared that Robert should have the lands which he held in France. That William should be the King of England. And that Henry should have no land at all, but only a chest of gold.

So it happened in the end very much as the wise men had foretold. Robert, the Short Stocking, was bold and reckless, like the hawk, which he so much admired. He lost all the lands that his father had left him and was at last shut up in prison, where he was kept until he died.

William Rufus was so overbearing and cruel that he was feared and hated by all his people. He led a wicked life and was killed by one of his own men while hunting in the forest.

And Henry, the Handsome Scholar, had not only the chest of gold for his own. But by and by, he became the King of England and the ruler of all the lands that his father had had in France.

Written Summation

Model Practice 1

There was once a great king of England who was called William the Conqueror. He had three sons.

The first who came into the room was Robert. He was a tall, willful lad and was nicknamed Short Stocking.

Model Practice 2

Model Practice 3

The White Ship
1068 - 1135
from Fifty Famous Stories Retold
by James Baldwin

King Henry, the Handsome Scholar, had one son, named William, whom he dearly loved. The young man was noble and brave, and everybody hoped that he would some day be the King of England.

One summer Prince William went with his father across the sea to look after their lands in France. They were welcomed with joy by all their people there, and the young prince was so gallant and kind, that he won the love of all who saw him.

But at last, the time came for them to go back to England. The king, with his wise men and brave knights, set sail early in the day; but Prince William with his younger friends waited a little while. They had had so joyous a time in France that they were in no great haste to tear them-selves away.

Then they went on board of the ship, which was waiting to carry them home. It was a beautiful ship with white sails and white masts, and it had been fitted up on purpose for this voyage.

The sea was smooth. The winds were fair. And no one thought of danger. On the ship, everything had been arranged to make the trip a pleasant one. There was music and dancing, and everybody was merry and glad.

The sun had gone down before the white-winged vessel was fairly out of the bay. But what of that? The moon was at its full, and it would give light enough; and before the dawn of the morrow, the narrow sea would be crossed. And so the prince, and the young people who were with him, gave themselves up to merri-ment and feasting and joy.

The earlier hours of the night passed by; and then there was a cry of alarm on deck. A moment afterward, there was a great crash. The ship had struck upon a rock. The water rushed in. She was sinking. Ah, where now were those who had lately been so heart-free and glad?

Every heart was full of fear. No one knew what to do. A small boat was quickly launched, and the prince with a few of his bravest friends leaped into it. They pushed off just as the ship was beginning to settle beneath the waves. Would they be saved?

They had rowed hardly ten yards from the ship, when there was a cry from among those that were left behind.

"Row back!" cried the prince. "It is my little sister. She must be saved!"

The men did not dare to disobey. The boat was again brought along side of the sinking vessel. The prince stood up, and held out his arms for his sister. At that moment, the ship gave a great lurch forward into the waves. One shriek of terror was heard, and then all was still save the sound of the moaning waters.

Ship and boat, prince and princess, and all the gay company that had set sail from France went down to the bottom together. One man clung to a floating plank and was saved the next day. He was the only person left alive to tell the sad story.

When King Henry heard of the death of his son, his grief was more than he could bear. His heart was broken. He had no more joy in life; and men say that no one ever saw him smile again.

Here is a poem about him that your teacher may read to you, and perhaps, after a while, you may learn it by heart.

HE NEVER SMILED AGAIN

The bark that held the prince went down,
The sweeping waves rolled on;
And what was England's glorious crown
To him that wept a son?
He lived, for life may long be borne
Ere sorrow breaks its chain:
Why comes not death to those who mourn?
He never smiled again.
There stood proud forms before his throne,
The stately and the brave;
But who could fill the place of one,—
That one beneath the wave?
Before him passed the young and fair,
In pleasure's reckless train;
But seas dashed o'er his son's bright hair—
He never smiled again.
He sat where festal bowls went round;
He heard the minstrel sing;
He saw the tour-ney's victor crowned
Amid the knightly ring.
A murmur of the restless deep
Was blent with every strain,
A voice of winds that would not sleep—
He never smiled again.
Hearts, in that time, closed o'er the trace
Of vows once fondly poured,
And strangers took the kinsman's place
At many a joyous board;
Graves which true love had bathed with tears
Were left to heaven's bright rain;
Fresh hopes were born for other years—
He never smiled again!

Mrs. Hemans.

Written Summation

Model Practice 1

One summer Prince William went with his father across the sea to look after their lands in France.

The sea was smooth. The winds were fair. And no one thought of danger.

Model Practice 2

Model Practice 3

The King and His Hawk
1162 - 1227
from Fifty Famous Stories Retold
by James Baldwin

Genghis Khan was a great king and warrior. He led his army into China and Persia, and he conquered many lands. In every country, men told about his daring deeds; and they said that since Alexander the Great there had been no king like him.

One morning when he was home from the wars, he rode out into the woods to have a day's sport. Many of his friends were with him. They rode out gayly, carrying their bows and arrows. Behind them came the servants with the hounds.

It was a merry hunting party. The woods rang with their shouts and laughter. They expected to carry much game home in the evening.

On the king's wrist sat his favorite hawk, for in those days hawks were trained to hunt. At a word from their masters, they would fly high up into the air, and look around for prey. If they chanced to see a deer or a rabbit, they would swoop down upon it swift as any arrow.

All day long, Genghis Khan and his huntsmen rode through the woods. But they did not find as much game as they expected.

Toward evening, they started for home. The king had often ridden through the woods, and he knew all the paths. So while the rest of the party took the nearest way, he went by a longer road through a valley between two mountains.

The day had been warm, and the king was very thirsty. His pet hawk had left his wrist and flown away. It would be sure to find its way home.

The king rode slowly along. He had once seen a spring of clear water near this pathway. If he could only find it now! But the hot days of summer had dried up all the mountain brooks.

At last, to his joy, he saw some water trickling down over the edge of a rock. He knew that there was a spring farther up. In the wet season, a swift stream of water always poured down here, but now it came only one drop at a time.

The king leaped from his horse. He took a little silver cup from his hunting bag. He held it so as to catch the slowly falling drops.

It took a long time to fill the cup, and the king was so thirsty that he could hardly wait. At last, it was nearly full. He put the cup to his lips and was about to drink.

All at once, there was a whirring sound in the air, and the cup was knocked from his hands. The water was spilled upon the ground.

The king looked up to see who had done this thing. It was his pet hawk.

The hawk flew back and forth a few times and then alighted among the rocks by the spring.

The king picked up the cup and again held it to catch the trickling drops.

This time he did not wait so long. When the cup was half-full, he lifted it toward his mouth. But before it had touched his lips, the hawk swooped down again and knocked it from his hands.

And now the king began to grow angry. He tried again, and for the third time the hawk kept him from drinking.

The king was now very angry indeed.

"How do you dare to act so?" he cried. "If I had you in my hands, I would wring your neck!"

Then he filled the cup again. But before he tried to drink, he drew his sword.

"Now, Sir Hawk," he said, "this is the last time."

He had hardly spoken, before the hawk swooped down and knocked the cup from his hand. But the king was looking for this. With a quick sweep of the sword, he struck the bird as it passed.

The next moment the poor hawk lay bleeding and dying at its master's feet.

"That is what you get for your pains," said Genghis Khan.

But when he looked for his cup, he found that it had fallen between two rocks, where he could not reach it.

"At any rate, I will have a drink from that spring," he said to himself.

With that, he began to climb the steep bank to the place from which the water trickled. It was hard work, and the higher he climbed, the thirstier he became.

At last, he reached the place. There indeed was a pool of water, but what was that lying in the pool and almost filling it? It was a huge, dead snake of the most poisonous kind.

The king stopped. He forgot his thirst. He thought only of the poor dead bird lying on the ground below him.

"The hawk saved my life!" he cried. "And how did I repay him? He was my best friend, and I have killed him."

He clambered down the bank. He took the bird up gently and laid it in his hunting bag. Then he mounted his horse and rode swiftly home. He said to himself,—

"I have learned a sad lesson today; and that is, never to do anything in anger."

Written Summation

Model Practice 1

The king rode slowly along. He had once seen a spring of clear water near this pathway. If he could only find it now!

The king stopped. He forgot his thirst. He thought only of the poor dead bird lying on the ground below him.

Model Practice 2

Model Practice 3

King John and the Abbot
1166 - 1216
from <u>Fifty Famous Stories Retold</u>
by James Baldwin

I. THE THREE QUESTIONS.

There was once a king of England whose name was John. He was a bad king, for he was harsh and cruel to his people. And so long as he could have his own way, he did not care what became of other folks. He was the worst king that England ever had.

Now, there was in the town of Canterbury a rich old abbot who lived in grand style in a great house called the Abbey. Every day a hundred noble men sat down with him to dine, and fifty brave knights, in fine velvet coats and gold chains, waited upon him at his table.

When King John heard of the way in which the abbot lived, he made up his mind to put a stop to it. So he sent for the old man to come and see him.

"How now, my good abbot?" he said. "I hear that you keep a far better house than I. How dare you do such a thing? Don't you know that no man in the land ought to live better than the king? And I tell you that no man shall."

"O king!" said the abbot, "I beg to say that I am spending nothing but what is my own. I hope that you will not think ill of me for making things pleasant for my friends and the brave knights who are with me."

"Think ill of you?" said the king. "How can I help but think ill of you? All that there is in this broad land is mine by right. And how do you dare to put me to shame by living in grander style than I? One would think that you were trying to be king in my place."

"Oh, do not say so!" said the abbot. "For I—"

"Not another word!" cried the king. "Your fault is plain, and unless you can answer me three questions, your head shall be cut off, and all your riches shall be mine."

"I will try to answer them, O king!" said the abbot.

"Well, then," said King John, "as I sit here with my crown of gold on my head, you must tell me to within a day just how long I shall live. Secondly, you must tell me how soon I shall ride round the whole world. And lastly, you shall tell me what I think."

"O king!" said the abbot, "these are deep, hard questions, and I cannot answer them just now. But if you will give me two weeks to think about them, I will do the best that I can."

"Two weeks you shall have," said the king; "but if then you fail to answer me, you shall lose your head, and all your lands shall be mine."

The abbot went away very sad and in great fear. He first rode to Oxford. Here was a great school, called a university, and he wanted to see if any of the wise professors could help him. But they shook their heads and said that there was nothing about King John in any of their books.

Then the abbot rode down to Cambridge, where there was another university. But not one of the teachers in that great school could help him.

At last, sad and sorrowful, he rode toward home to bid his friends and his brave knights good-by. For now he had not a week to live.

II. THE THREE ANSWERS.

As the abbot was riding up the lane, which led to his grand house, he met his shepherd going to the fields.

"Welcome home, good master!" cried the shepherd. "What news do you bring us from great King John?"

"Sad news, sad news," said the abbot, and then he told him all that had happened.

"Cheer up, cheer up, good master," said the shepherd. "Have you never yet heard that a fool may teach a wise man wit? I think I can help you out of your trouble."

"You help me!" cried the abbot "How? How?"

"Well," answered the shepherd, "you know that everybody says that I look just like you, and that I have sometimes been mistaken for you. Lend me your servants, horse, and gown. I will go up to London and see the king. If nothing else can be done, I can at least die in your place."

"My good shepherd," said the abbot, "you are very, very kind, and I have a mind to let you try your plan. But if the worst comes to the worst, you shall not die for me. I will die for myself."

So the shepherd got ready to go at once. He dressed himself with great care. Over his shepherd's coat, he threw the abbot's long gown, and he borrowed the abbot's cap and golden staff. When all was ready, no one in the world would have thought that he was not the great man himself. Then he mounted his horse and, with a great train of servants, set out for London.

Of course, the king did not know him.

"Welcome, Sir Abbot!" he said. "It is a good thing that you have come back. But, prompt as you are, if you fail to answer my three questions, you shall lose your head."

"I am ready to answer them, O king!" said the shepherd.

"Indeed, indeed!" said the king, and he laughed to himself. "Well, then, answer my first question: How long shall I live? Come, you must tell me to the very day."

"You shall live," said the shepherd, "until the day that you die, and not one day longer. And you shall die when you take your last breath, and not one moment before."

The king laughed.

"You are witty, I see," he said. "But we will let that pass, and say that your answer is right. And now tell me how soon I may ride round the world."

"You must rise with the sun," said the shepherd, "and you must ride with the sun until it rises again the next morning. As soon as you do that, you will find that you have ridden round the world in twenty-four hours."

The king laughed again. "Indeed," he said, "I did not think that it could be done so soon. You are not only witty, but you are wise, and we will let this answer pass. And now comes my third and last question: What do I think?"

"That is an easy question," said the shepherd. "You think that I am the Abbot of Canterbury. But, to tell you the truth, I am only his poor shepherd, and I have come to beg your pardon for him and for me." And with that, he threw off his long gown.

The king laughed loud and long.

"A merry fellow you are," said he, "and you shall be the Abbot of Canterbury in your master's place."

"O king! That cannot be," said the shepherd, "for I can neither read nor write."

"Very well, then," said the king, "I will give you something else to pay you for this merry joke. I will give you four pieces of silver every week as long as you live. And when you get home, you may tell the old abbot that you have brought him a free pardon from King John."

Written Summation

Model Practice 1

Lend me your servants,

horse, and gown. I will

go up to London and see

the king.

"Indeed, indeed!" said the king, and he laughed to himself. "How long shall I live? Come, you must tell me to the very day."

Model Practice 2 (adapted from the original)

Model Practice 3

The Shepherd Boy Painter

1267 - 1337
from Fifty Famous People
by James Baldwin

One day a traveler was walking through a part of Italy where a great many sheep were pasturing. Near the top of a hill he saw a little shepherd boy who was lying on the ground while a flock of sheep and lambs were grazing around him.

As he came nearer, he saw that the boy held a charred stick in his hand, with which he was drawing something on a flat rock. The lad was so much interested in his work that he did not see the stranger.

The stranger bent over him and looked at the picture he had made on the rock. It was the picture of a sheep, and it was drawn so well that the stranger was filled with astonishment.

"What is your name, my boy?" he said.

The lad was startled. He jumped to his feet and looked up at the kind gentleman.

"My name is Giotto," he answered.

"What is your father's name?"

"Bondone."

"And whose sheep are these?"

"They belong to the rich man who lives in the big white house there among the trees. My father works in the field, and I take care of the sheep."

"How would you like to live with me, Giotto? I would teach you how to draw pictures of sheep and horses, and even of men," said the stranger.

The boy's face beamed with delight. "I should like to learn to do that—oh, ever so much!" he answered. "But I must do as father says."

"Let us go and ask him," said the stranger.

The stranger's name was Cimabue. He was the most famous painter of the time. His pictures were known and admired in every city of Italy.

Bondone was surprised when Cimabue offered to take his little boy to Florence and teach him to be a great painter.

"I know that the lad can draw pictures wonderfully well," he said. "He does not like to do anything else. Perhaps he will do well with you. Yes, you may take him."

In the city of Florence little Giotto saw some of the finest pictures in the world. He learned so fast that he could soon paint as well as Cimabue himself.

One day Cimabue was painting the picture of a man's face. Night came on before he had finished it. "I will leave it till morning," he said; "then the light will be better."

In the morning, when he looked at the picture, he saw a fly on the man's nose. He tried to brush it off, but it remained there. It was only a painted fly.

"Who has done this?" he cried. He was angry, and yet he was pleased.

Little Giotto came out from a corner, trembling and ashamed. "I did it, master," he said. "It was a good place for a fly, and I never thought of spoiling your picture."

He expected to be punished. But Cimabue only praised him for his great skill. "There are few men who can draw so good a picture of a fly," he said.

This happened six hundred years ago, in the city of Florence in Italy. The shepherd boy became a very famous painter and the friend of many famous men.

Written Summation

Model Practice 1

The stranger's name
was Cimabue. He was
the most famous painter
of the time.

In the morning, when he looked at the picture, he saw a fly on the man's nose. He tried to brush it off, but it remained there.

Model Practice 2

Model Practice 3

The Hunted King, Robert I king of the Scots
1274 1329
from Fifty Famous People
by James Baldwin

What boy or girl has not heard the story of King Robert Bruce and the spider? I will tell you another story of the same brave and famous king. He had fought a battle with his enemies, the English. His little army had been beaten and scattered. Many of his best friends had been killed or captured. The king himself was obliged to hide in the wild woods while his foes hunted for him with hounds.

For many days, he wandered through rough and dangerous places, waded across muddy rivers, and climbed over rugged mountains. Sometimes two or three faithful friends were with him. Sometimes he was alone. Sometimes his enemies were very close.

Late one evening he came to a little farmhouse in a lonely valley. He walked in without knocking. A woman was sitting alone by the fire.

"May a poor traveler find rest and shelter here for the night?" he asked. The woman answered, "All travelers are welcome for the sake of one, and you are welcome."

"Who is that one?" asked the king.

"That is Robert the Bruce," said the woman. "He is the rightful lord of this country. He is now being hunted with hounds, but I hope soon to see him king over all Scotland."

"Since you love him so well," said the king, "I will tell you something. I am Robert the Bruce."

"You!" cried the woman in great surprise. "Are you the Bruce, and are you all alone?"

"My men have been scattered," said the king, "and therefore there is no one with me."

"That is not right," said the brave woman. "I have two sons who are gallant and trustworthy. They shall go with you and serve you."

So she called her two sons. They were tall and strong young men, and they gladly promised to go with the king and help him.

The king sat down by the fire, and the woman hurried to get things ready for supper. The two young men got down their bows and arrows, and all were busy making plans for the next day.

Suddenly a great noise was heard outside. They listened. They heard the tramping of horses and the voices of a number of men.

"The English! The English!" said the young men.

"Be brave, and defend your king with your lives," said their mother.

Then some one outside called loudly, "Have you seen King Robert the Bruce pass this way?"

"That is my brother Edward's voice," said the king. "These are friends, not enemies."

The door was thrown open, and he saw a hundred brave men, all ready to give him aid. He forgot his hunger; he forgot his weariness. He began to ask about his enemies who had been hunting him.

"I saw two hundred of them in the village below us," said one of his officers. "They are resting there for the night and have no fear of danger from us. If you have a mind to make haste, we may surprise them."

"Then let us mount and ride," said the king.

The next minute they were off. They rushed suddenly into the village. They routed the king's enemies and scattered them.

And Robert the Bruce was never again obliged to hide in the woods or to run from savage hounds. Soon he became the real king and ruler of all Scotland

Written Summation

Model Practice 1

Sometimes two or three

faithful friends were

with him. Sometimes he

was alone. Sometimes

his enemies were very

close.

So she called her two sons.
They were tall and strong young men,
and they gladly promised to go with
the king and help him.

Model Practice 2

Model Practice 3

The Black Douglas

1286 - 1330
from Fifty Famous Stories Retold
by James Baldwin

In Scotland, in the time of King Robert Bruce, there lived a brave man whose name was Douglas. His hair and beard were black and long, and his face was tanned and dark. And for this reason, people nicknamed him the Black Douglas. He was a good friend of the king, and one of his strongest helpers.

In the war with the English, who were trying to drive Bruce from Scotland, the Black Douglas did many brave deeds; and the English people became very much afraid of him. By and by, the fear of him spread all through the land. Nothing could frighten an English lad more than to tell him that the Black Douglas was not far away. Women would tell their children, when they were naughty, that the Black Douglas would get them. This would make them very quiet and good.

There was a large castle in Scotland which the English had taken early in the war. The Scottish soldiers wanted very much to take it again. So the Black Douglas and his men went one day to see what they could do. It happened to be a holiday, and most of the English soldiers in the castle were eating and drinking and having a merry time. But they had left watchmen on the wall to see that the Scottish soldiers did not come upon them unawares; and so they felt quite safe.

In the evening, when it was growing dark, the wife of one of the soldiers went up on the wall with her child in her arms. As she looked over into the fields below the castle, she saw some dark objects moving toward the foot of the wall. In the dusk, she could not make out what they were. And so she pointed them out to one of the watchmen.

"Pooh, pooh!" said the watchman. "Those are nothing to frighten us. They are the farmer's cattle, trying to find their way home. The farmer himself is enjoying the holiday, and he has forgotten to bring them in. If the Douglas should happen this way before morning, he will be sorry for his carelessness."

But the dark objects were not cattle. They were the Black Douglas and his men, creeping on hands and feet toward the foot of the castle wall. Some of them were dragging ladders behind them through the grass. They would soon be climbing to the top of the wall. None of the English soldiers dreamed that they were within many miles of the place.

The woman watched them until the last one had passed around a corner out of sight. She was not afraid. For in the darkening twilight, they looked indeed like cattle. After a little while, she began to sing to her child:—

"Hush ye, hush ye, little pet ye,
Hush ye, hush ye, do not fret ye,
The Black Douglas shall not get ye."

All at once, a gruff voice was heard behind her, saying, "Don't be so sure about that!"

She looked around, and there stood the Black Douglas himself. At the same moment, a Scottish soldier climbed off a ladder and leaped upon the wall. Then there came another and another and another, until the wall was covered with them. Soon there was hot fighting in every part of the castle. But the English were so taken by surprise that they could not do much. Many of them were killed. And in a little while, the Black Douglas and his men were the masters of the castle, which by right belonged to them.

As for the woman and her child, the Black Douglas would not suffer any one to harm them. After a while, they went back to England; and whether the mother made up any more songs about the Black Douglas I cannot tell.

Written Summation

Model Practice 1

In the dusk, she could
not make out what they
were. And so she pointed
them out to one of the
watchmen.

The woman watched them until the last one had passed around a corner out of sight. She was not afraid.

Model Practice 2

Model Practice 3

The Story of William Tell

1307
from Fifty Famous Stories Retold
by James Baldwin

The people of Switzerland were not always free and happy as they are today. Many years ago a proud tyrant, whose name was Gessler, ruled over them and made their lot a bitter one indeed.

One day this tyrant set up a tall pole in the public square and put his own cap on the top of it. Then he gave orders that every man who came into the town should bow down before it. But there was one man named William Tell who would not do this. He stood up straight with folded arms, and laughed at the swinging cap. He would not bow down to Gessler himself.

When Gessler heard of this, he was very angry. He was afraid that other men would disobey, and that soon the whole country would rebel against him. So he made up his mind to punish the bold man.

William Tell's home was among the mountains, and he was a famous hunter. No one in all the land could shoot with bow and arrow so well as he. Gessler knew this, and so he thought of a cruel plan to make the hunter's own skill bring him to grief. He ordered that Tell's little boy should be made to stand up in the public square with an apple on his head. Then he bade Tell shoot the apple with one of his arrows.

Tell begged the tyrant not to have him make this test of his skill. What if the boy should move? What if the bowman's hand should tremble? What if the arrow should not carry true?

"Will you make me kill my boy?" he said.

"Say no more," said Gessler. "You must hit the apple with your one arrow. If you fail, my soldiers shall kill the boy before your eyes."

Then, without another word, Tell fitted the arrow to his bow. He took aim and let it fly. The boy stood firm and still. He was not afraid, for he had all faith in his father's skill.

The arrow whistled through the air. It struck the apple fairly in the center and carried it away. The people who saw it shouted with joy.

As Tell was turning away from the place, an arrow, which he had hidden under his coat, dropped to the ground.

"Fellow!" cried Gessler, "what mean you with this second arrow?"

"Tyrant!" was Tell's proud answer; "this arrow was for your heart if I had hurt my child."

And there is an old story, that, not long after this, Tell did shoot the tyrant with one of his arrows; and thus he set his country free.

Written Summation

Model Practice 1

One day this tyrant

set up a tall pole in the

public square and put his

own cap on the top of it.

The arrow whistled through the air. It struck the apple fairly in the center and carried it away. The people who saw it shouted with joy.

Model Practice 2

Model Practice 3

"TRY, TRY AGAIN!"
1336 - 1405
from Fifty Famous People
by James Baldwin

There was once a famous ruler of Tartary whose name was Tamerlane. Like Alexander the Great, he wished to become the master of the whole world. So he raised a great army and made war against other countries. He conquered many kings and burned many cities.

But at last his army was beaten; his men were scattered; and Tamerlane fled alone from the field of battle.

For a long time he wandered in fear from place to place. His foes were looking for him. He was in despair. He was about to lose all hope.

One day he was lying under a tree, thinking of his misfortunes. He had now been a wanderer for twenty days. He could not hold out much longer. Suddenly he saw a small object creeping up the trunk of the tree. He looked more closely and saw that it was an ant. The ant was carrying a grain of wheat as large as itself.

As Tamerlane looked, he saw that there was a hole in the tree only a little way above, and that this was the home of the ant. "You are a brave fellow, Mr. Ant," he said. "But you have a heavy load to carry."

Just as he spoke, the ant lost its footing and fell to the ground. But it still held on to the grain of wheat.

A second time it tried to carry its load up the rough trunk of the tree, and a second time it failed.

Tamerlane watched the brave little insect. It tried three times, four times, a dozen times, twenty times, but always with the same result.

Then it tried the twenty-first time. Slowly, one little step at a time, it crept up across the rough place where it had slipped and fallen so often. The next minute it ran safely into its home, carrying its precious load. "Well done!" said

Tamerlane. "You have taught me a lesson. I, too, will try, try again, till I succeed."

And this he did.

Of what other story does this remind you?

Written Summation

Model Practice 1

Just as he spoke, the ant lost its footing and fell to the ground. But it still held on to the grain of wheat.

Tamerlane watched the brave little insect. It tried three times, four times, a dozen times, twenty times, but always with the same result.

Model Practice 2

Model Practice 3

Arnold Winkelried

1386
from Fifty Famous Stories Retold
by James Baldwin

A great army was marching into Switzerland. If it should go much farther, there would be no driving it out again. The soldiers would burn the towns, they would rob the farmers of their grain and sheep, and they would make slaves of the people.

The men of Switzerland knew all this. They knew that they must fight for their homes and their lives. And so they came from the mountains and valleys to try what they could do to save their land. Some came with bows and arrows, some with scythes and pitchforks, and some with only sticks and clubs.

But their foes kept in line as they marched along the road. Every soldier was fully armed. As they moved and kept close together, nothing could be seen of them but their spears and shields and shining armor. What could the poor country people do against such foes as these?

"We must break their lines," cried their leader; "for we cannot harm them while they keep together."

The bowmen shot their arrows, but they glanced off from the soldiers' shields. Others tried clubs and stones, but with no better luck. The lines were still unbroken. The soldiers moved steadily onward; their shields lapped over one another; their thousand spears looked like so many long bristles in the sunlight. What cared they for sticks and stones and huntsmen's arrows?

"If we cannot break their ranks," said the Swiss, "we have no chance for fight, and our country will be lost!"

Then a poor man, whose name was Arnold Winkelried, stepped out.

"On the side of yonder mountain," said he, "I have a happy home. There my wife and children wait for my return. But they will not see me again, for this day I will give my life for my country. And to you, my friends, do your duty, and Switzerland shall be free."

With these words, he ran forward. "Follow me!" he cried to his friends. "I will break the lines, and then let every man fight as bravely as he can."

He had nothing in his hands, neither club nor stone nor other weapon. But he ran straight onward to the place where the spears were thickest.

"Make way for liberty!" he cried, as he dashed right into the lines.

A hundred spears were turned to catch him upon their points. The soldiers forgot to stay in their places. The lines were broken. Arnold's friends rushed bravely after him. They fought with whatever they had in hand. They snatched spears and shields from their foes. They had no thought of fear. They only thought of their homes and their dear native land. And they won at last.

Such a battle no one ever knew before. But Switzerland was saved, and Arnold Winkelried did not die in vain.

Written Summation

Model Practice 1

Some came with bows and arrows, some with scythes and pitchforks, and some with only sticks and clubs.

They snatched spears and shields from their foes. They had no thought of fear. They only thought of their homes and their dear native land.

Model Practice 2

Model Practice 3

The Horseshoe Nails
1452 - 1485
from Fifty Famous People
by James Baldwin

A blacksmith was shoeing a horse.

"Shoe him quickly, for the king wishes to ride him to battle," said the groom who had brought him.

"Do you think there will be a battle?" asked the blacksmith.

"Most certainly, and very soon, too," answered the man. "The king's enemies are even now advancing, and all are ready for the fight. Today will decide whether Richard or Henry shall be king of England."

The smith went on with his work. From a bar of iron, he made four horseshoes. These he hammered and shaped and fitted to the horse's feet. Then he began to nail them on.

But after he had nailed on two shoes, he found that he had not nails enough for the other two.

"I have only six nails," he said, "and it will take a little time to hammer out ten more."

"Oh, well," said the groom, "won't six nails do? Put three in each shoe. King Richard will be impatient."

"Three nails in each shoe will hold them on," said the smith. "Yes, I think we may risk it."

So he quickly finished the shoeing, and the groom hurried to lead the horse to the king.

The battle had been raging for some time. King Richard rode hither and thither, cheering his men and fighting his foes. His enemy, Henry, who wished to be king, was pressing him hard.

Far away, at the other side of the field, King Richard saw his men falling back. Without his help they would soon be beaten. So he spurred his horse to ride to their aid.

He was hardly halfway across the stony field when one of the horse's shoes flew off. The horse was lamed on a rock. Then another shoe came off. The horse stumbled, and his rider was thrown heavily to the ground.

Before the king could rise, his frightened horse, although lame, had galloped away. The king looked and saw that his soldiers were beaten and that the battle was everywhere going against him.

He waved his sword in the air. He shouted, "A horse! A horse! My kingdom for a horse."

But there was no horse for him. His soldiers were intent on saving themselves. They could not give him any help.

The battle was lost. King Richard was lost. Henry became king of England.

> "For the want of a nail the shoe was lost;
> For the want of a shoe the horse was lost;
> For the want of a horse the battle was lost;
> For the failure of battle the kingdom was lost; —
> And all for the want of a horseshoe nail."

Richard the Third was one of England's worst kings. Henry, the Duke of Richmond, made war upon him and defeated him in a great battle.

Written Summation

Model Practice 1

"Oh, well," said the

groom, "won't six nails do?

Put three in each shoe.

King Richard will be

impatient."

So he quickly finished his shoeing, and the groom hurried to lead the horse to the king.

Model Practice 2

Model Practice 3

King Edward and his Bible

1537-1553
from Parker's Second Reader
by Mrs. L.H. Sigourney.

I will tell you a little story about a young and good king. He was king of England more than two hundred and eighty years ago. His name was Edward. And because there had been five kings before him of the name of Edward, he was called Edward the Sixth.

He was only nine years old when he began to reign. He was early taught to be good, by pious teachers. And he loved to do what they told him would please God. He had a great reverence for the Bible, which he knew contained the words of his Father in heaven.

Once, when he was quite a young child, he was playing with some children about his own age. He wished much to reach something, which was above his head. To assist him, they laid a large, thick book in a chair for him to step on. Just as he was putting his foot upon it, he discovered it to be the Bible.

Drawing back, he took it in his arms, kissed it, and returned it to its place. Turning to his little playmates, he said, with a serious face, "Shall I dare to tread under my feet that which God has commanded me to keep in my heart?"

This pious king never forgot his prayers. Though the people with whom he lived were continually anxious to amuse him and show him some new thing, they never could induce him to omit his daily devotions.

One day he heard that one of his teachers was sick. Immediately, he retired to pray for him. Coming from his prayers, he said, with a cheerful countenance, "I think there is hope that he will recover. I have this morning earnestly begged of God to spare him to us."

After his teacher became well, he was told of this. And he very much loved the young king for remembering him in his prayers.

Edward the Sixth died when he was sixteen years old. He was beloved by all for his goodness and piety. His mind was calm and serene in his sickness.

If you are not tired of my story, I will tell you part of a prayer which he said often, when on his dying bed.

"My Lord God, if thou wilt deliver me from this miserable life, take me among thy chosen. Yet not my will, but thy will be done. Lord, I commit my spirit unto thee. Thou knowest how happy it were for me to be with thee. Yet, if thou shouldst send me life and health, grant that I may truly serve thee."

Children, you should do like King Edward, reverence your Bible, and love to pray to God.

Written Summation

Model Practice 1

One day he heard that one of his teachers was sick. Immediately, he retired to pray for him.

Edward the Sixth died when he was sixteen years old. He was beloved by all for his goodness and piety.

Model Practice 2

Model Practice 3

Sir Humphrey Gilbert
1539 - 1583
from <u>Fifty Famous Stories Retold</u>
by James Baldwin

More than three hundred years ago, there lived in England a brave man whose name was Sir Humphrey Gilbert. At that time, there were no white people in this country of ours. The land was covered with forests; and where there are now great cities and fine farms, there were only trees and swamps among which roamed the Indians and wild beasts.

Sir Humphrey Gilbert was one of the first men who tried to make a settlement in America. Twice did he bring men and ships over the sea, and twice did he fail and sail back for England. The second time, he was on a little ship called the <u>Squirrel</u>. Another ship, called the <u>Golden Hind</u>, was not far away. When they were three days from land, the wind failed, and the ships lay floating on the waves. Then at night, the air grew very cold. A breeze sprang up from the east. Great white icebergs came drifting around them. In the morning, the little ships were almost lost among the floating mountains of ice. The men on the <u>Hind</u> saw Sir Humphrey sitting on the deck of the <u>Squirrel</u> with an open book in his hand. He called to them and said,—

"Be brave, my friends! We are as near heaven on the sea as on the land."

Night came again. It was a stormy night with mist and rain. All at once, the men on the <u>Hind</u> saw the lights on board of the <u>Squirrel</u> go out. The little vessel, with brave Sir Humphrey and all his brave men, was swallowed up by the waves.

Written Summation

Model Practice 1

When they were three days from land, the wind failed, and the ships lay floating on the waves.

Great white icebergs came drifting around them. In the morning, the little ships were almost lost among the floating mountains of ice.

Model Practice 2

Model Practice 3

Sir Walter Raleigh

1552 - 1618
from Fifty Famous Stories
by James Baldwin

There once lived in England a brave and noble man whose name was Walter Raleigh. He was not only brave and noble, but he was also handsome and polite. And for that reason, the queen made him a knight and called him Sir Walter Raleigh.

When Raleigh was a young man, he was one day walking along a street in London. At that time, the streets were not paved, and there were no sidewalks. Raleigh was dressed in very fine style, and he wore a beautiful scarlet cloak thrown over his shoulders.

As he passed along, he found it hard work to keep from stepping in the mud and soiling his handsome new shoes. Soon he came to a puddle of muddy water, which reached, from one side of the street to the other. He could not step across. Perhaps he could jump over it.

As he was thinking what he should do, he happened to look up. Who was it coming down the street on the other side of the puddle?

It was Elizabeth, the Queen of England, with her train of gentlewomen and waiting maids. She saw the dirty puddle in the street. She saw the handsome young man with the scarlet cloak, standing by the side of it. How was she to get across?

Young Raleigh, when he saw who was coming, forgot about himself. He thought only of helping the queen. There was only one thing that he could do, and no other man would have thought of that.

He took off his scarlet cloak and spread it across the puddle. The queen could step on it now, as on a beautiful carpet.

She walked across. She was safely over the ugly puddle, and her feet had not touched the mud. She paused a moment, and thanked the young man.

As she walked onward with her train, she asked one of the gentlewomen, "Who is that brave gentleman who helped us so handsomely?"

"His name is Walter Raleigh," said the gentlewomen.

"He shall have his reward," said the queen.

Not long after that, she sent for Raleigh to come to her palace.

The young man went, but he had no scarlet cloak to wear. Then, while all the great men and fine ladies of England stood around, the queen made him a knight. And from that time, he was known as Sir Walter Raleigh, the queen's favorite.

Sir Walter Raleigh and Sir Humphrey Gilbert, about whom I have already told you, were half-brothers.

When Sir Humphrey made his first voyage to America, Sir Walter was with him. After that, Sir Walter tried several times to send men to this country to make a settlement.

But those whom he sent found only great forests, and wild beasts, and savage Indians. Some of them went back to England; some of them died for want of food; and some of them were lost in the woods. At last Sir Walter gave up trying to get people to come to America.

But he found two things in this country that the people of England knew very little about. One was the potato, and the other was tobacco.

If you should ever go to Ireland, you may be shown the place where Sir Walter planted the few potatoes that he carried over from America. He told his friends how the Indians used them for food; and he proved that they would grow in the Old World as well as in the New.

Sir Walter had seen the Indians smoking the leaves of the tobacco plant. He thought that he would do the same, and he carried some of the leaves to England. Englishmen had never used tobacco before that time; and all who saw Sir Walter puffing away at a roll of leaves thought that it was a strange sight.

One day as he was sitting in his chair and smoking, his servant came into the room. The man saw the smoke curling over his master's head, and he thought that he was on fire.

He ran out for some water. He found a pail that was quite full. He hurried back and threw the water into Sir Walter's face. Of course, the fire was all put out.

After that a great many men learned to smoke. And now tobacco is used in all countries of the world. It would have been well if Sir Walter Raleigh had let it alone.

Written Summation

Model Practice 1

He found two things
in this country that the
people of England knew
very little about. One
was the potato, and the
other was tobacco.

He ran out for some water. He found a pail that was quite full. He hurried back and threw the water into Sir Walter's face.

Model Practice 2

Model Practice 3

Which Was the King?
1553 - 1610
from Fifty Famous People
by James Baldwin

One day King Henry the Fourth of France was hunting in a large forest. Towards evening, he told his men to ride home by the main road while he went by another way that was somewhat longer.

As he came out of the forest, by the roadside he saw a little boy, who seemed to be watching for someone.

"Well, my boy," said the king, "are you looking for your father?"

"No, sir," answered the boy. "I am looking for the king. They say he is hunting in the woods, and perhaps will ride out this way. So I'm waiting to see him."

"Oh, if that is what you wish," said King Henry, "get up behind me on the horse, and I'll take you to the place where you will see him."

The boy got up at once and sat behind the king. The horse cantered briskly along, and king and boy were soon quite well acquainted.

"They say that King Henry always has a number of men with him," said the boy; "how shall I know which is he?"

"Oh, that will be easy enough," was the answer. "All the other men will take off their hats, but the king will keep his on."

"Do you mean that the one with his hat on will be the king?"

"Certainly."

Soon they came into the main road where a number of the king's men were waiting. All the men seemed amused when they saw the boy, and as they rode up, they greeted the king by taking off their hats.

"Well, my boy," said King Henry, "which do you think is the king?"

"I don't know," answered the boy; "but it must be either you or I, for we both have our hats on."

Written Summation

Model Practice 1

On Feb. 27, 1594

King Henry IV was finally

crowned the King of

France.

"No, sir," answered the boy. "I am looking for the king. They say he is hunting in the woods. So I'm waiting to see him."

Model Practice 2

Model Practice 3

Sir Philip Sidney

1554 - 1586
from <u>Fifty Famous Stories</u>
by James Baldwin

A cruel battle was being fought. The ground was covered with dead and dying men. The air was hot and stifling. The sun shone down without pity on the wounded soldiers lying in the blood and dust.

One of these soldiers was a nobleman, whom everybody loved for his gentleness and kindness. Yet now he was no better off than the poorest man in the field. He had been wounded and would die; and he was suffering much with pain and thirst.

When the battle was over, his friends hurried to his aid. A soldier came running with a cup in his hand.

"Here, Sir Philip," he said, "I have brought you some clear, cool water from the brook. I will raise your head so that you can drink."

The cup was placed to Sir Philip's lips. How thankfully he looked at the man who had brought it! Then his eyes met those of a dying soldier who was lying on the ground close by. The wistful look in the poor man's face spoke plainer than words.

"Give the water to that man," said Sir Philip quickly. Then, pushing the cup toward him, he said, "Here, my comrade, take this. Thy need is greater than mine."

What a brave, noble man he was! The name of Sir Philip Sidney will never be forgotten. For it was the name of a Christian gentleman who always had the good of others in his mind. Was it any wonder that everybody wept when it was heard that he was dead?

It is said, that, on the day when he was carried to the grave, every eye in the land was filled with tears. Rich and poor, high and low, all felt that they had lost a friend; all mourned the death of the kindest, gentlest man that they had ever known.

Written Summation

Model Practice 1

The air was hot and stifling. The sun shone down without pity on the wounded soldiers lying in the blood and dust.

What a brave, noble man he was! The name of Sir Philip Sidney will never be forgotten.

Model Practice 2

Model Practice 3

CHAPTER II

English Tales

How Jack Went to Seek His Fortune
from English Fairy Tales
by Joseph Jacobs

Once on a time there was a boy named Jack, and one morning he decided to seek his fortune.

He hadn't gone very far before he met a cat. "Where are you going, Jack?" said the cat.

"I am going to seek my fortune."

"May I go with you?"

"Yes," said Jack, "the more the merrier."

So on they went, jiggelty jolt, jiggelty jolt.

They went a little further and they met a dog.

"Where are you going, Jack?" said the dog.

"I am going to seek my fortune."

"May I go with you?"

"Yes," said Jack, "the more the merrier."

So on they went, jiggelty jolt, jiggelty jolt. They went a little further and they met a goat.

"Where are you going, Jack?" said the goat.

"I am going to seek my fortune."

"May I go with you?"

"Yes," said Jack, "the more the merrier."

So on they went, jiggelty jolt, jiggelty jolt.

They went a little further and they met a bull.

"Where are you going, Jack?" said the bull.

"I am going to seek my fortune."

"May I go with you?"

"Yes," said Jack, "the more the merrier."

So on they went, jiggelty jolt, jiggelty jolt.

They went a little further and they met a rooster.

"Where are you going, Jack?" said the rooster.

"I am going to seek my fortune."

"May I go with you?"

"Yes," said Jack, "the more the merrier."

So on they went, jiggelty jolt, jiggelty jolt.

Well, they went on till it was about dark, and they began to think of some place where they could spend the night. About this time, they came in sight of a house, and Jack told them to keep still while he went up and looked in through the window. And there were some robbers counting over their money. Then Jack went back and told them to wait till he gave the word, and then to make all the noise they could. So when they were all ready Jack gave the word, and the cat mewed, and the dog barked, and the goat bleated, and the bull bellowed, and the rooster crowed, and all together they made such a dreadful noise that it frightened the robbers all away.

Then they went in and took possession of the house. Jack was afraid the robbers would come back in the night, so when it came time to go to bed he put the cat in the rocking-chair, and he put the dog under the table, and he put the goat upstairs, and he put the bull down cellar, and the rooster flew up on to the roof, and Jack went to bed.

By-and-by the robbers saw it was all dark, and they sent one man back to the house to look after their money. Before long, he came back in a great fright and told them his story.

"I went back to the house," said he, "and went in and tried to sit down in the rocking-chair, and there was an old woman knitting, and she stuck her knitting-needles into me." That was the cat, you know.

"I went to the table to look after the money and there was a shoemaker under the table, and he stuck his awl into me." That was the dog, you know.

"I started to go upstairs, and there was a man up there threshing, and he knocked me down with his flail." That was the goat, you know.

"I started to go down cellar, and there was a man down there chopping wood, and he knocked me up with his axe." That was the bull, you know.

"But I shouldn't have minded all that if it hadn't been for that little fellow on top of the house, who kept a-hollering, 'Chuck him up to me-e! Chuck him up to me-e!'" Of course that was the cock-a-doodle-do.

Written Summation

Model Practice 1 (adapted from the original)

So on they went,

jiggelty jolt, jiggelty jolt.

They went a little further,

and they met a goat.

He hadn't gone very far before he met a cat. "Where are you going, Jack?" said the cat.

Model Practice 2

Model Practice 3

Jack Hannaford
from English Fairy Tales
by Joseph Jacobs

There was an old soldier who had been long in the wars—so long, that he was quite out-at-elbows, and he did not know where to go to find a living. So he walked up moors, down glens, till at last he came to a farm, from which the good man had gone away to market. The wife of the farmer was a very foolish woman, who had been a widow when he married her; the farmer was foolish enough, too, and it is hard to say which of the two was the more foolish. When you've heard my tale, you may decide.

Now before the farmer goes to market says he to his wife: "Here is ten pounds all in gold, take care of it till I come home." If the man had not been a fool he would never have given the money to his wife to keep. Well, off he went in his cart to market, and the wife said to herself: "I will keep the ten pounds quite safe from thieves." So she tied it up in a rag, and she put the rag up the parlor chimney.

"There," said she, "no thieves will ever find it now; that is quite sure."

Jack Hannaford, the old soldier, came and rapped at the door.

"Who is there?" asked the wife.

"Jack Hannaford."

"Where do you come from?"

"Paradise."

"Lord a' mercy! And maybe you've seen my old man there," alluding to her former husband.

"Yes, I have."

"And how was he a-doing?" asked the goody.

"But middling; he cobbles old shoes, and he has nothing but cabbage for victuals."

"Deary me!" exclaimed the woman. "Didn't he send a message to me?"

"Yes, he did," replied Jack Hannaford. "He said that he was out of leather, and his pockets were empty, so you were to send him a few shillings to buy a fresh stock of leather."

"He shall have them. Bless his poor soul!" And away went the wife to the parlor chimney, and she pulled the rag with the ten pounds in it from the chimney, and she gave the whole sum to the soldier, telling him that her old man was to use as much as he wanted, and to send back the rest.

It was not long that Jack waited after receiving the money. He went off as fast as he could walk.

Presently the farmer came home and asked for his money. The wife told him that she had sent it by a soldier to her former husband in Paradise, to buy him leather for cobbling the shoes of the saints and angels of Heaven. The farmer was very angry, and he swore that he had never met with such a fool as his wife. But the wife said that her husband was a greater fool for letting her have the money.

There was no time to waste words. So the farmer mounted his horse and rode off after Jack Hannaford. The old soldier heard the horse's hoofs clattering on the road behind him. He knew it must be the farmer pursuing him. So he lay down on the ground, and shading his eyes with one hand, looked up into the sky, and pointed heavenwards with the other hand.

"What are you about there?" asked the farmer, pulling up.

"Lord save you!" exclaimed Jack: "I've seen a rare sight."

"What was that?"

"A man going straight up into the sky, as if he were walking on a road."

"Can you see him still?"

"Yes, I can."

"Where?"

"Get off your horse and lie down."

"If you will hold the horse."

Jack did so readily.

"I cannot see him," said the farmer.

"Shade your eyes with your hand, and you'll soon see a man flying away from you."

Sure enough, he did so, for Jack leaped on the horse, and rode away with it. The farmer walked home without his horse.

"You are a bigger fool than I am," said the wife; "for I did only one foolish thing, and you have done two."

Written Summation

Model Practice 1

It was not long that Jack waited after receiving the money. He went off as fast as he could walk.

There was no time to waste words. So the farmer mounted his horse and rode off after Jack Hannaford.

Model Practice 2

Model Practice 3

Lazy Jack
from English Fairy Tales
by Joseph Jacobs

Once upon a time there was a boy whose name was Jack. He lived with his mother on a common. They were very poor, and the old woman made her living by spinning. But Jack was so lazy. He would do nothing but bask in the sun in the summer and sit by the corner of the hearth in the winter. So they called him Lazy Jack. His mother could not get him to do anything for her. At last she told him, one Monday, that if he did not begin to work for his porridge, she would turn him out to get his living as he could.

This roused Jack. And he went out and hired himself for the next day to a neighboring farmer for a penny. But as he was coming home, he lost it passing over a brook.

"You stupid boy," said his mother. "You should have put it in your pocket."

"I'll do so another time," replied Jack.

On Wednesday, Jack went out again and hired himself to a cow keeper. The cow keeper gave him a jar of milk for his day's work. Jack took the jar. He put it into the large pocket of his jacket and spilled it all, long before he got home.

"Dear me!" said the old woman. "You should have carried it on your head."

"I'll do so another time," said Jack.

So on Thursday, Jack hired himself again to a farmer, who agreed to give him a cream cheese for his services. In the evening, Jack took the cheese, and went home with it on his head. By the time he got home, the cheese was all spoiled. Part of it being lost, and part matted with his hair.

"You stupid lout," said his mother. "You should have carried it very carefully in your hands."

"I'll do so another time," replied Jack.

On Friday, Lazy Jack again went out. He hired himself to a baker, who would give him nothing for his work but a large tomcat. Jack took the cat and began carrying it very carefully in his hands. But in a short time, the cat scratched him so much that he was compelled to let it go.

When he got home, his mother said to him, "You silly fellow, you should have tied it with a string and dragged it along after you."

"I'll do so another time," said Jack.

So on Saturday, Jack hired himself to a butcher. The butcher rewarded him with the handsome present of a shoulder of mutton. Jack took the mutton, tied it to a string, and trailed it along after him in the dirt. By the time he had got home, the meat was completely spoiled. His mother was this time quite out of patience with him. For the next day was Sunday, and she was obliged to make do with cabbage for her dinner.

"You ninney-hammer," said she to her son. "You should have carried it on your shoulder."

"I'll do so another time," replied Jack.

On the next Monday, Lazy Jack went once more. He hired himself to a cattle-keeper, who gave him a donkey for his trouble. Jack found it hard to hoist the donkey on his shoulders. But at last, he did it and began walking slowly home with his prize. Now it happened, that in the course of his journey, there lived a rich man with his only daughter. She was a beautiful girl, but deaf and dumb. She had never laughed in her life. The doctors said she would never speak till somebody made her laugh. This young lady happened to be looking out of the window when Jack was passing with the donkey on his shoulders, with the legs sticking up in the air. The sight was so comical and strange that she burst out into a great fit of laughter. And she immediately recovered her speech and hearing. Her father was overjoyed. He fulfilled his promise by marrying her to Lazy Jack, who was thus made a rich gentleman. They lived in a large house, and Jack's mother lived with them in great happiness until she died.

Written Summation

Model Practice 1

He would do nothing but bask in the sun in the summer and sit by the corner of the hearth in the winter. So they called him Lazy Jack.

On Wednesday, Jack went out again and hired himself to a cow keeper. The cow keeper gave him a jar of milk for his day's work.

Model Practice 2

Model Practice 3

II-19

Little Red Riding Hood

from English Fairy Tales
by Flora Annie Steel

Once upon a time, there was a little girl who was called little Red Riding Hood. She was quite small, and she always wore a red cloak with a big red hood to it, which her grandmother had made for her.

Now one day her mother, who had been churning and baking cakes, said to her, "My dear, put on your red cloak with the hood to it. And take this cake, and this pot of butter to your Grannie, and ask how she is, for I hear she is ailing."

Now little Red Riding Hood was very fond of her grandmother who made her so many nice things. So she put on her cloak joyfully and started on her errand. But her grandmother lived some way off. And to reach the cottage, little Red Riding Hood had to pass through a vast lonely forest. However, some woodcutters were at work in it. So little Red Riding Hood was not so very much alarmed when she saw a great big wolf coming toward her, because she knew that wolves were cowardly things.

And sure enough, the wolf only stopped and asked her politely where she was going. But for the woodcutters, he would surely have eaten little Red Riding Hood.

"I am going to see Grannie, take her this cake and this pot of butter, and ask how she is," says little Red Riding Hood."

"Does she live a very long way off?" asked the wolf craftily.

"Not so very far if you go by the straight road," replied little Red Riding Hood. "You only have to pass the mill and the first cottage on the right is Grannie's. But I am going by the wood-path because there are such a lot of nuts and flowers and butterflies."

"I wish you good luck," says the wolf politely. "Give my respects to your grandmother and tell her I hope she is quite well."

And with that, he trotted off. But instead of going his way, he turned back, took the straight road to the old woman's cottage, and knocked at the door.

Rap! Rap! Rap!

"Who's there?" asked the old woman, who was in bed.

"Little Red Riding Hood," sang out the wolf, making his voice as shrill as he could. "I've come to bring dear Grannie a pot of butter and a cake from mother, and to ask how you are."

"Pull the bobbin, and the latch will go up," said the old woman, well satisfied.

So the wolf pulled the bobbin, the latch went up, and oh my! It wasn't a minute before he had gobbled up old Grannie, for he had had nothing to eat for a week.

Then he shut the door, put on Grannie's nightcap, and rolled himself well up in the bed.

By and by along came little Red Riding Hood, who had been amusing herself by gathering nuts, running after butterflies, and picking flowers.

So she knocked at the door. Rap! Rap! Rap!

"Who's there?" says the wolf, making his voice as soft as he could.

Now little Red Riding Hood heard the voice was very gruff, but she thought her grandmother had a cold. So she said, "Little Red Riding Hood with a pot of butter and a cake from mother to ask how you are."

"Pull the bobbin, and the latch will go up."

So little Red Riding Hood pulled the bobbin, the latch went up, and there, she thought, was her grandmother in the bed; for the cottage was so dark, one could not see well. Besides, the crafty wolf turned his face to the wall at first. And he made his voice as soft as soft as he could, when he said:

"Come and kiss me, my dear."

Then little Red Riding Hood took off her cloak and went to the bed.

"Oh, Grandmamma, Grandmamma," says she, "what big arms you've got!"

"All the better to hug you with," says he.

"But Grandmamma, Grandmamma, what big legs you have!"

"All the better to run with, my dear."

"Oh, Grandmamma, Grandmamma, what big ears you've got!"

"All the better to hear with, my dear."

"But Grandmamma, Grandmamma, what big eyes you've got!"

"All the better to see you with, my dear!"

"Oh, Grandmamma, Grandmamma, what big teeth you've got!"

"All the better to eat you with, my dear!" says that wicked, wicked wolf, and with that, he gobbled up little Red Riding Hood.

Written Summation

Model Practice 1

Then he shut the door,

put on Grannie's nightcap,

and rolled himself well up

in the bed.

Little Red Riding Hood had been amusing herself by gathering nuts, running after butterflies, and picking flowers.

Model Practice 2

Model Practice 3

The Magpie's Nest
from English Fairy Tales
by Joseph Jacobs

Once upon a time, all the birds of the air came to the magpie and asked her to teach them how to build nests. For the magpie is the cleverest bird of all at building nests. So she put all the birds round her and began to show them how to do it. First of all, she took some mud and made a sort of round cake with it.

"Oh, that's how it's done," said the thrush; and away it flew, and so that's how thrushes build their nests.

Then the magpie took some twigs and arranged them round in the mud.

"Now I know all about it," said the blackbird, and off he flew. And that's how the blackbirds make their nests to this very day.

Then the magpie put another layer of mud over the twigs.

"Oh that's quite obvious," said the wise owl, and away it flew; and owls have never made better nests since.

After this, the magpie took some twigs and twined them round the outside.

"The very thing!" said the sparrow, and off he went; so sparrows make rather slovenly nests to this day.

Then Madge Magpie took some feathers and stuff and lined the nest very comfortably with it.

"That suits me," cried the starling, and off it flew; and very comfortable nests have starlings.

So it went on, every bird taking away some knowledge of how to build nests with none of them waiting until the end. Meanwhile, Madge Magpie went on working and working, without looking up. Finally, the only bird that remained was the turtledove. But the turtledove hadn't paid any attention all along. It only kept on saying its silly cry, "Take two, Taffy, take two-o-o-o."

At last the magpie heard this just as she was putting a twig across. So she said: "One's enough."

But the turtledove kept on, saying, "Take two, Taffy, take two-o-o-o."

Then the magpie got angry and said, "One's enough I tell you."

Still the turtledove cried, "Take two, Taffy, take two-o-o-o."

At last, and at last, the magpie looked up and saw none near her but the silly turtledove. Then she got rare angry and flew away and refused to tell the birds how to build nests again. And that is why different birds build their nests differently.

Written Summation

Model Practice 1

Finally, the only bird that remained was the turtledove. But the turtledove hadn't paid any attention all along.

"Now I know all about it," said the blackbird, and off he flew. And that's how the blackbirds make their nests to this very day.

Model Practice 2

Model Practice 3

The Miller's Guest
from a Child's World Reader
by Hetty Browne, Sarah Withers, W.K. Tate

A hunter who had ridden ahead in the chase was lost. The sun went down, and darkness fell upon the forest. The hunter blew his horn, but no answer came. What should he do?

At last, he heard the sound of horse's hoofs. Someone was coming. Was it friend or foe? The hunter stood still, and soon a miller rode out into the moonlight.

"Pray, good fellow, be so kind as to tell me the way to Nottingham," said the hunter.

"Nottingham? Why should you be going to Nottingham? The king and his court are there. It is not a place for the likes of you," replied the miller.

"Well, well, perhaps you are right, good miller," said the hunter. "And yet who knows? I'll wager that the king is no better man than I am. However, it is getting late, and lodging I must have. Will you give me shelter for the night?"

"Nay, nay, not so fast," said the miller. "Stand forth and let me see if you are a true man. Many thieves wear fine clothes these days."

The hunter stepped forward. "Well, and what do you think of me?" he asked gayly. "Will you not give a stranger lodging?"

"How do I know that you have one penny in your purse?" asked the miller. "You may carry your all on your back, for aught I know. I've heard of lords who are like that."

"True, good miller, but I have gold. If it be forty pence, I will pay it," said the hunter.

"If you are a true man, and have the pence, then lodging you may have. My good wife may not like it, but we'll see," said the miller.

"Good!" cried the hunter. "And here's my hand on it."

"Nay, nay, not so fast," replied the miller. "I must know you better before I shake hands. None but an honest man's hand will I take."

"Some day, my good miller," replied the hunter, "I hope to have you take my hand in yours. Proud will I be when the day comes."

And so to the miller's house they went. The miller again looked at the stranger and said, "I like his face well. He may stay with us, may he not, good wife?"

"Yes, he is a handsome youth, but it's best not to go too fast," said the good wife. "He may be a runaway servant. Let him show his passport, and all shall be well."

The hunter bowed low, and said, "I have no passport, good dame, and I never was any man's servant. I am but a poor courtier who has lost his way. Pray give me lodging for the night. Your kindness I will surely repay."

Then the wife whispered to the miller, "The youth is of good manners and to turn him out would be sin."

"Yea, a well-mannered youth—and one who knows his betters when he sees them," the miller replied. "Let the lad stay."

"Well, young man," said the wife, "you are welcome here; and well lodged you shall be, though I do say it myself. You shall have a fresh bed with good brown sheets."

"Aye," said the miller, "and you shall sleep with our own son Richard."

Then they all sat down to supper—such a supper: pudding, apple pie, and good things of all kinds. Then at a wink from the miller, the wife brought out a venison pasty.

"Eat!" said the miller. "This is dainty food."

"Faith!" cried the hunter, "I never before ate such meat."

"Pshaw!" said Richard. "We eat this every day."

"Every day? Where do you buy it?"

"Oh, never a penny pay we. In merry Sherwood Forest, we find it. Now and then, you see, we make bold with the king's deer."

"Then I think that it is venison," said the hunter.

"To be sure. Any fool would know that," replied Richard; "but say nothing about it. We would not have the king hear of it."

"I'll keep your secret," said the hunter. "Don't fear. The king shall never know more than he knows now."

And so the evening passed merrily. It was late when the guest sought his bed, but right soundly did he sleep.

The next morning the miller, the good wife, and Richard came out to see the hunter on his way. Just then, a party of nobles rode up.

"There's the king!" cried one.

"Pardon, your majesty!" cried another, and all fell upon their knees before the hunter.

The miller stood shaking and quaking, and for once his wife could not speak. The king, with a grave face, drew his sword, but not a word did he say.

The terrified miller threw himself at his ruler's feet, crying out for mercy. Again, the sword was raised, and down it fell, but lightly, upon the miller's shoulder, and the king said:

"Your kind courtesy I will repay; so I here dub thee Knight. Rise, Sir John of Mansfield."

For many a day the miller and his wife told of the night the king spent with them. And for many a day the king told of the time he was taken for a thief and ate of his own deer in the miller's house.

Written Summation

Model Practice 1

At last, he heard the

sound of horse's hoofs.

Someone was coming.

Was it friend or foe?

"I'll keep your secret," said the hunter. "Don't fear. The king shall never know more than he knows now."

Model Practice 2

Model Practice 3

The Old Woman and Her Pig
from English Fairy Tales
by Joseph Jacobs

An old woman was sweeping her house, and she found a little crooked sixpence. "What," said she, "shall I do with this little sixpence? I will go to market, and buy a little pig."

As she was coming home, she came to a stile: but the piggy wouldn't go over the stile.

She went a little further, and she met a dog. She said to the dog, "Dog! Bite pig! Piggy won't go over the stile, and I shan't get home tonight." But the dog wouldn't.

She went a little further, and she met a stick. So she said, "Stick! Stick! Beat dog! Dog won't bite pig. Piggy won't get over the stile. And I shan't get home tonight." But the stick wouldn't.

She went a little further, and she met a fire. So she said, "Fire! Fire! Burn stick; stick won't beat dog; dog won't bite pig; piggy won't get over the stile; and I shan't get home tonight." But the fire wouldn't.

She went a little further, and she met some water. So she said: "Water, water! Quench fire; fire won't burn stick; stick won't beat dog; dog won't bite pig; piggy won't get over the stile; and I shan't get home tonight." But the water wouldn't.

She went a little further, and she met an ox. So she said, "Ox! Ox! Drink water! Water won't quench fire. Fire won't burn stick. Stick won't beat dog. Dog won't bite pig. Piggy won't get over the stile. And I shan't get home tonight." But the ox wouldn't.

She went a little further, and she met a butcher. So she said: "Butcher! Butcher! Kill ox; ox won't drink water; water won't quench fire; fire won't burn stick; stick won't beat dog; dog won't bite pig;

Piggy won't get over the stile; and I shan't get home tonight." But the butcher wouldn't.

She went a little further, and she met a rope. So she said: "Rope! Rope! Hang butcher; butcher won't kill ox; ox won't drink water; water won't quench fire; fire won't burn stick; stick won't beat dog; dog won't bite pig; piggy won't get over the stile; and I shan't get home tonight." But the rope wouldn't.

She went a little further, and she met a rat. So she said: "Rat! Rat! Gnaw rope; rope won't hang butcher; butcher won't kill ox; ox won't drink water; water won't quench fire; fire won't burn stick; stick won't beat dog; dog won't bite pig; piggy won't get over the stile; and I shan't get home tonight." But the rat wouldn't.

She went a little further, and she met a cat. So she said: "Cat! Cat! Kill rat; rat won't gnaw rope; rope won't hang butcher; butcher won't kill ox; ox won't drink water; water won't quench fire; fire won't burn stick; stick won't beat dog; dog won't bite pig; piggy won't get over the stile; and I shan't get home tonight." But the cat said to her, "If you will go to yonder cow, and fetch me a saucer of milk, I will kill the rat." So away went the old woman to the cow.

But the cow said to her: "If you will go to yonder hay-stack, and fetch me a handful of hay, I'll give you the milk." So away went the old woman to the haystack and she brought the hay to the cow.

As soon as the cow had eaten the hay, she gave the old woman the milk. And away she went with it in a saucer to the cat.

As soon as the cat had lapped up the milk, the cat began to kill the rat; the rat began to gnaw the rope; the rope began to hang the butcher; the butcher began to kill the ox; the ox began to drink the water; the water began to quench the fire; the fire began to burn the stick; the stick began to beat the dog; the dog began to bite the pig; the little pig in a fright jumped over the stile, and so the old woman got home that night.

Written Summation

Model Practice 1 (adapted from the original)

She said to the dog, "Dog!

Bite pig! Piggy won't go

over the stile, and I shall

not get home tonight."

But the dog wouldn't.

As soon as the cow had eaten the hay, she gave the old woman the milk. And away she went with it in a saucer to the cat.

Model Practice 2

Model Practice 3

Other Wise Men of Gotham
from Fifty Famous Stories Retold
by James Baldwin

One day, news was brought to Gotham that the king was coming that way, and that he would pass through the town. This did not please the men of Gotham at all. They hated the king, for they knew that he was a cruel, bad man. If he came to their town, they would have to find food and lodging for him and his men; and if he saw anything that pleased him, he would be sure to take it for his own. What should they do?

They met together to talk the matter over.

"Let us chop down the big trees in the woods, so that they will block up all the roads that lead into the town," said one of the wise men.

"Good!" said all the rest.

So they went out with their axes. And soon all the roads and paths to the town were filled with logs and brush. The king's horsemen would have a hard time of it getting into Gotham. They would either have to make a new road, or give up the plan altogether, and go on to some other place.

When the king came and saw that the road had been blocked up, he was very angry.

"Who chopped those trees down in my way?" he asked of two country lads that were passing by.

"The men of Gotham," said the lads.

"Well," said the king, "go and tell the men of Gotham that I shall send my sheriff into their town and have all their noses cut off."

The two lads ran to the town as fast as they could and made known what the king had said.

Everybody was in great fright. The men ran from house to house, carrying the news and asking one another what they should do.

"Our wits have kept the king out of the town," said one; "and so now our wits must save our noses."

"True, true!" said the others. "But what shall we do?"

Then one, whose name was Dobbin, and who was thought to be the wisest of them all, said, "Let me tell you something. Many a man has been punished because he was wise, but I have never heard of any one being harmed because he was a fool. So, when the king's sheriff comes, let us all act like fools."

"Good, good!" cried the others. "We will all act like fools."

It was no easy thing for the king's men to open the roads; and while they were doing it, the king grew tired of waiting and went back to London. But very early one morning, the sheriff with a party of fierce soldiers rode through the woods, and between the fields, toward Gotham. Just before they reached the town, they saw a queer sight. The old men were rolling big stones up the hill, and all the young men were looking on, and grunting very loudly.

The sheriff stopped his horses and asked what they were doing.

"We are rolling stones uphill to make the sun rise," said one of the old men.

"You foolish fellow!" said the sheriff. "Don't you know that the sun will rise without any help?"

"Ah! Will it?" said the old man. "Well, I never thought of that. How wise you are!"

"And what are *you* doing?" said the sheriff to the young men.

"Oh, we do the grunting while our fathers do the working," they answered.

"I see," said the sheriff. "Well, that is the way the world goes everywhere." And he rode on toward the town.

He soon came to a field where a number of men were building a stonewall.

"What are you doing?" he asked.

"Why, master," they answered, "there is a cuckoo in this field, and we are building a wall around it so as to keep the bird from straying away."

"You foolish fellows!" said the sheriff. "Don't you know that the bird will fly over the top of your wall, no matter how high you build it?"

"Why, no," they said. "We never thought of that. How very wise you are!"

The sheriff next met a man who was carrying a door on his back.

"What are you doing?" he asked.

"I have just started on a long journey," said the man.

"But why do you carry that door?" asked the sheriff.

"I left my money at home."

"Then why didn't you leave the door at home too?"

"I was afraid of thieves. And you see, if I have the door with me, they can't break it open and get in."

"You foolish fellow!" said the sheriff. "It would be safer to leave the door at home, and carry the money with you."

"Ah, would it, though?" said the man. "Now, I never thought of that. You are the wisest man that I ever saw."

Then the sheriff rode on with his men; but every one that they met was doing some silly thing.

"Truly I believe that the people of Gotham are all fools," said one of the horsemen.

"That is true," said another. "It would be a shame to harm such simple people."

"Let us ride back to London, and tell the king all about them," said the sheriff.

"Yes, let us do so," said the horsemen.

So they went back, and told the king that Gotham was a town of fools; and the king laughed, and said that if that was the case, he would not harm them, but would let them keep their noses.

Written Summation

Model Practice 1

So they went out with their axes. And soon all the roads and paths to the town were filled with logs and brush.

Everybody was in great fright. The men ran from house to house, carrying the news and asking one another what they should do.

Model Practice 2

Model Practice 3

Saddle to Rags
from <u>A Child's World Reader</u>
by Hetty Browne, Sarah Withers, W.K. Tate

This story I'm going to sing,
I hope it will give you content,
Concerning a silly old man
That was going to pay his rent,
With a till-a-dill, till-a-dill-dill,
Till-a-dill, dill-a-dill, dee,
Sing fol-de-dill, dill-de-dill, dill,
Fol-de-dill, dill-de-dill, dee.

A silly old man said to his wife one day, "Well, 'tis time I paid my rent. The landlord has been away for a year and a day, but now he is back, and I must pay for twelve months."

"Yes, it's twice forty pounds that is due, and it should be paid," said the good wife. "So much money in the house keeps me from sleeping at night."

"Well, I'll bridle old Tib, and away we shall go," said the old man. "Right glad I'll be, too, to be rid of the gold."

The silly old man bridled old Tib and saddled her too. And away they started. As he was jogging along, a stranger came riding up on a fine horse with fine saddlebags.

"Good morning, old man," said the stranger.

"Good morning," said the old man.

"How far are you going?"

"To tell the truth, kind sir, I am going just two miles," said the old man.

"And where are you going?" asked the stranger.

"I am going to pay my rent, kind sir," said the old man. "I am but a silly old man who farms a piece of ground. My rent for a half-year is forty pounds; but my landlord has been away for a year, and now I owe him eighty pounds. Right glad I am to pay it."

"Eighty pounds! That is indeed a large sum," cried the stranger, "and you ought not to tell anybody you carry so much. There are many thieves about, and you might be robbed."

"Oh, never mind!" said the old man. "I do not fear thieves. My money is safe in my saddle bags, on which I ride."

So they rode along most pleasantly.

When they came to a thick wood, the stranger pulled out a pistol and said, "Stand still, and give me your money."

"Nay," said the old man. "The money is for my landlord. I will not give it to you."

"Your money or your life!"

"Well, if you will have it, you can go for it," cried the old man. Then he threw his old saddlebags over a hedge.

The thief dismounted and said, "Stand here and hold my horse while I go over the hedge. You are silly, but surely you can do that."

The thief climbed through the hedge. When he was on the other side, the old man got on the thief's horse, and away he galloped.

"Stop, stop!" cried the thief. "And half of my share you shall have."

"Nay," cried the man. "I think I'll go on. I'd rather have what's in your bag."

And away he galloped, riding as he never rode before.

The thief thought there must be something in the old man's bags; so with his big rusty knife he chopped them into rags. But no money did he find, for the silly old man was not so silly as he seemed. His money was in his pocket.

The old man rode on to his landlord's home and paid his rent. Then he opened the thief's bag, which was glorious to behold. There were five hundred pounds in gold and silver.

"Where did you get the silver?" asked the landlord. "And where did you get the gold?"

"I met a proud fool on the way," said the old man with a laugh. "I swapped horses with him, and he gave me this to boot."

"Well, well! But you're too old to go about with so much money," said the landlord.

"Oh, I think no one would harm a silly old man like me," said the farmer, as he rode away.

The old man went home by a narrow lane, and there he spied Tib tied to a tree.

"The stranger did not like his trade, I fear," said he. "So I think I'll take Tib home."

The old man went home much richer than when he left. When she heard the story, the wife danced and sang for glee. "'Tis hard to fool my old man," said she.

—ENGLISH BALLAD (Adapted).

Written Summation

Model Practice 1

The silly old man bridled old Tib and saddled her too. And away they started.

"Well, if you will have it, you can go for it," cried the old man. Then he threw his old saddlebags over a hedge.

Model Practice 2

Model Practice 3

The Shoemaker and the Elves
from A Beacon Second Reader
by James H. Fassett

A shoemaker and his wife lived in a little house on the edge of a wood. They were very, very poor, and each day they grew poorer and poorer. At last, there was nothing left in the house but leather for one pair of shoes.

"I will cut out this last pair of shoes," the shoemaker said to his wife. "Tomorrow I will sew them and peg them."

So he cut out the leather and left it on his bench. The next morning he went into his shop to make the shoes. What did he see? A pair of shoes, all nicely made and ready to be sold.

The stitches were so fine and the shoes so well made that they were quickly sold. With the money, the poor shoemaker bought leather for two pairs of shoes.

Then he said to his wife, "I will cut out the leather for two pairs of shoes. Tomorrow I will sew them and peg them."

So he cut out the leather for the shoes and left it on his bench.

The next morning when he went into his shop to make the shoes, what did he find! Yes, there were two pairs of shoes already made. The work was so well done that those shoes were also sold very quickly. With the money, the poor shoemaker bought enough leather for four pairs of shoes. Those he also cut out and left upon his bench.

The next morning he found four pairs of beautiful shoes, all well made.

And so it went on and on. Instead of being a very poor shoemaker, he became a very rich shoemaker. His shoes were so well made that even the queen herself wore them.

At last, the shoemaker said to his wife, "We must find out who makes the shoes."

So one bright moonlight night, they hid behind a curtain, where they could watch the bench and not be seen.

Just on the stroke of midnight, two little elves jumped through the window. They went skipping and dancing up to the bench. Sitting cross-legged, they took up the leather and began to work.

How their needles flew back and forth, back and forth! How their little hammers beat rap-a-tap-tap, rap-a-tap-tap!

Almost before the shoemaker and his wife could think, the work was all done. The tiny elves ran about, skipping and dancing, skipping and dancing. Then, whisk! Quick as a wink, they were gone.

The next morning the good shoemaker said to his wife, "What can we do for those dear little elves?"

"I should like very much to make some clothes for them," said his wife. "They were almost naked."

"If you will make their coats, I will make them some shoes," said the shoemaker. "Their little feet were bare."

When the clothes and shoes were ready, they were put upon the bench. The shoemaker and his wife again hid behind the curtain.

Just as before, when the clock struck twelve, in jumped the tiny elves. They went skipping and dancing, skipping and dancing, to their work.

They saw the little coats, the tiny stockings, and the neat little shoes. They clapped their hands for joy. Then, slipping on their clothes, they skipped, hand in hand, out of the window.

The shoemaker and his wife never saw the little elves again, but after that night, good luck seemed always to be with them.

Written Summation

Model Practice 1

The next morning he went
into his shop to make the
shoes. What did he see?
A pair of shoes, all nicely
made and ready to be sold.

They saw the little coats, the tiny stockings, and the neat little shoes. They clapped their hands for joy.

Model Practice 2

Model Practice 3

A Story of Robin Hood
from Fifty Famous Stories Retold
by James Baldwin

In the rude days of King Richard and King John, there were many great woods in England. The most famous of these was Sherwood Forest, where the king often went to hunt deer. In this forest, there lived a band of daring men called outlaws.

They had done something that was against the laws of the land and had been forced to hide themselves in the woods to save their lives. There they spent their time in roaming about among the trees, in hunting the king's deer, and in robbing rich travelers that came that way.

There were nearly a hundred of these outlaws, and their leader was a bold fellow called Robin Hood. They were dressed in suits of green and armed with bows and arrows; and sometimes they carried long wooden lances and broadswords, which they knew how to handle well. Whenever they had taken anything, it was brought and laid at the feet of Robin Hood, whom they called their king. He then divided it fairly among them, giving to each man his just share.

Robin never allowed his men to harm anybody but the rich men who lived in great houses and did no work. He was always kind to the poor, and he often sent help to them. For that reason, the common people looked upon him as their friend.

Long after he was dead, men liked to talk about his deeds. Some praised him, and some blamed him. He was, indeed, a rude, lawless fellow; but at that time, people did not think of right and wrong as they do now.

A great many songs were made up about Robin Hood, and these songs were sung in the cottages and huts all over the land for hundreds of years afterward.

Here is a little story that is told in one of those songs: —

Robin Hood was standing one day under a green tree by the roadside. While he was listening to the birds among the leaves, he saw a young man passing by.

This young man was dressed in a fine suit of bright red cloth. And as he tripped gaily along the road, he seemed to be as happy as the day.

"I will not trouble him," said Robin Hood, "for I think he is on his way to his wedding."

The next day Robin stood in the same place. He had not been there long when he saw the same young man coming down the road. But he did not seem to be so happy this time. He had left his scarlet coat at home, and at every step, he sighed and groaned.

"Ah the sad day! The sad day!" he kept saying to himself.

Then Robin Hood stepped out from under the tree, and said, —

"I say, young man! Have you any money to spare for my merry men and me?"

"I have nothing at all," said the young man, "but five shillings and a ring."

"A gold ring?" asked Robin.

"Yes," said the young man, "it is a gold ring. Here it is."

"Ah, I see!" said Robin; "it is a wedding ring."

"I have kept it these seven years," said the young man; "I have kept it to give to my bride on our wedding day. We were going to be married yesterday. But her father has promised her to a rich old man whom she never saw. And now my heart is broken."

"What is your name?" asked Robin.

"My name is Allin-a-Dale," said the young man.

"What will you give me, in gold or fee," said Robin, "if I will help you win your bride again in spite of the rich old man to whom she has been promised?"

"I have no money," said Allin, "but I will promise to be your servant."

"How many miles is it to the place where the maiden lives?" asked Robin.

"It is not far," said Allin. "But she is to be married this very day, and the church is five miles away."

Then Robin made haste to dress himself as a harper; and in the afternoon, he stood in the door of the church.

"Who are you?" said the bishop, "and what are you doing here?"

"I am a bold harper," said Robin, "the best in the north country."

"I am glad you have come," said the bishop kindly. "There is no music that I like so well as that of the harp. Come in and play for us."

"I will go in," said Robin Hood; "but I will not give you any music until I see the bride and bridegroom."

Just then, an old man came in. He was dressed in rich clothing, but was bent with age and was feeble and gray. By his side walked a fair young girl. Her cheeks were very pale, and her eyes were full of tears.

"This is no match," said Robin. "Let the bride choose for herself."

Then he put his horn to his lips and blew three times. The very next minute, four and twenty men, all dressed in green and carrying long bows in their hands, came running across the fields. And as they marched into the church, all in a row, the foremost among them was Allin-a-Dale.

"Now whom do you choose?" said Robin to the maiden.

"I choose Allin-a-Dale," she said blushing.

"And Allin-a-Dale you shall have," said Robin; "and he that takes you from Allin-a-Dale shall find that he has Robin Hood to deal with."

And so the fair maiden and Allin-a-Dale were married then and there, and the rich old man went home in a great rage.

> "And thus having ended this merry wedding,
> The bride looked like a queen:
> And so they returned to the merry green wood,
> Amongst the leaves so green."

Written Summation

Model Practice 1

The next day Robin

stood in the same place.

He had not been there

long when he saw the

same young man coming

down the road.

But he did not seem to be so happy this time. He had left his scarlet coat at home, and at every step, he sighed and groaned.

Model Practice 2

Model Practice 3

The Story of the Three Little Pigs
by Unknown

Once upon a time, there was an old Sow with three little Pigs, and as she had not enough to keep them, she sent them out to seek their fortune.

The first that went off met a Man with a bundle of straw, and said to him, "Please, Man, give me that straw to build me a house"; which the Man did. And the little Pig built a house with it. Presently came along a Wolf and knocked at the door and said, "Little Pig, little Pig, let me come in."

To which the Pig answered, "No, no, no, not by the hair of my chinny chin chin."

"Then I'll huff and I'll puff, and I'll blow your house in!" said the Wolf. So he huffed and he puffed, and he blew his house in and ate up the little Pig.

The second Pig met a Man with a bundle of furze, and said, "Please, Man, give me that furze to build a house"; which the Man did, and the Pig built his house.

Then along came the Wolf and said, "Little Pig, little Pig, let me come in."

"No, no, no, not by the hair of my chinny chin chin."

"Then I'll puff and I'll huff, and I'll blow your house in!" So he huffed and he puffed, and he puffed and he huffed, and at last, he blew the house down and ate up the second little Pig.

The third little Pig met a Man with a load of bricks and said, "Please, Man, give me those bricks to build a house with"; so the Man gave him the bricks. And he built his house with them. So the Wolf came, as he did to the other little Pigs, and said, "Little Pig, little Pig, let me come in."

"No, no, no, not by the hair of my chinny chin chin."

"Then I'll huff and I'll puff, and I'll blow your house in."

Well, he huffed and he puffed, and he huffed and he puffed, and he puffed and he huffed; but he could not get the house down. When he found that he could not, with all his huffing and puffing, blow the house down, he said, "Little Pig, I know where there is a nice field of turnips."

"Where?" said the little Pig.

"Oh, in Mr. Smith's home field; and if you will be ready tomorrow morning, I will call for you. Then we will go together and get some for dinner."

"Very well," said the little Pig, "I will be ready. What time do you mean to go?"

"Oh, at six o'clock."

Well, the little Pig got up at five and got the turnips and was home again before six. When the Wolf came he said, "Little Pig, are you ready?"

"Ready!" said the little Pig, "I have been and come back again and got a nice potfull for dinner."

The Wolf felt very angry at this, but thought that he would be up to the little Pig somehow or other; so he said, "Little Pig, I know where there is a nice apple tree."

"Where?" said the Pig.

"Down at Merry Garden," replied the Wolf; "and if you will not deceive me I will come for you, at five o'clock tomorrow, and we will go together and get some apples."

Well, the little Pig woke at four the next morning and bustled up and went off for the apples, hoping to get back before the Wolf came. But he had farther to go and had to climb the tree, so that just as he was coming down from it, he saw the Wolf coming, which, as you may suppose, frightened him very much. When the Wolf came up he said, "Little Pig, what! Are you here before me? Are they nice apples?"

"Yes, very," said the little Pig; "I will throw you down one." And he threw it so far that, while the Wolf was gone to pick it up, the little Pig jumped down and ran home.

The next day the Wolf came again and said to the little Pig, "Little Pig, there is a Fair in the Town this afternoon. Will you go?"

"Oh, yes," said the Pig, "I will go. What time shall you be ready?"

"At three," said the Wolf.

So the little Pig went off before the time, as usual, and got to the Fair, and bought a butter churn, and was on his way home with it when he saw the Wolf coming. Then he could not tell what to do. So he got into the churn to hide, and in doing so turned it round, and it began to roll, and rolled down the hill with the Pig inside it, which frightened the Wolf so much that he ran home without going to the Fair.

He went to the little Pig's house and told him how frightened he had been by a great round thing which came down the hill past him.

Then the little Pig said, "Hah! I frightened you, did I? I had been to the Fair and bought a butter churn, and when I saw you I got into it and rolled down the hill."

Then the Wolf was very angry indeed and declared he would eat up the little Pig, and that he would get down the chimney after him.

When the little Pig saw what he was about, he hung on the pot full of water and made up a blazing fire and, just as the Wolf was coming down, took off the cover of the pot and in fell the Wolf. And the little Pig put on the cover again in an instant, boiled him up, ate him for supper, and lived happy ever after.

Written Summation

Model Practice 1

"Then I'll puff and I'll huff, and I'll blow your house in!" So he huffed and he puffed, and he puffed and he huffed.

Well, the little Pig got up at five and got the turnips and was home again before six.

Model Practice 2

Model Practice 3

Three Men of Gotham
from Fifty Famous Stories Retold
by James Baldwin

There is a town in England called Gotham, and many merry stories are told of the queer people who used to live there.

One-day two men of Gotham met on a bridge. Hodge was coming from the market, and Peter was going to the market.

"Where are you going?" said Hodge.

"I am going to the market to buy sheep," said Peter.

"Buy sheep?" said Hodge. "And which way will you bring them home?"

"I shall bring them over this bridge," said Peter.

"No, you shall not," said Hodge.

"Yes, but I will," said Peter.

"You shall not," said Hodge.

"I will," said Peter.

Then they beat with their sticks on the ground as though there had been a hundred sheep between them.

"Take care!" cried Peter. "Look out that my sheep don't jump on the bridge."

"I care not where they jump," said Hodge; "but they shall not go over it."

"But they shall," said Peter.

"Have a care," said Hodge; "for if you say too much, I will put my fingers in your mouth."

"Will you?" said Peter.

Just then, another man of Gotham came from the market with a sack of meal on his horse. He heard his neighbors quarreling about sheep; but he could see no sheep between them, and so he stopped and spoke to them.

"Ah, you foolish fellows!" he cried. "It is strange that you will never learn wisdom. Come here, Peter, and help me lay my sack on my shoulder."

Peter did so, and the man carried his meal to the side of the bridge.

"Now look at me," he said, "and learn a lesson." And he opened the mouth of the sack and poured all the meal into the river.

"Now, neighbors," he said, "Can you tell how much meal is in my sack?"

"There is none at all!" cried Hodge and Peter together.

"You are right," said the man; "and you that stand here and quarrel about nothing, having no more sense in your heads than I have meal in my sack!"

Written Summation

Model Practice 1

One day two men of Gotham met on a bridge. Hodge was coming from the market, and Peter was going to the market.

"Now look at me," he said, "and learn a lesson." And he opened the mouth of the sack and poured all the meal into the river.

Model Practice 2

Model Practice 3

Tom Thumb

from The Beacon Second Reader
by James H. Fassett.

In the days of King Arthur, there lived a wise man named Merlin. He knew all the fairies and where they lived. Even the fairy queen was a friend of his.

Once, while he was traveling, night overtook him in a deep forest. He rapped at the door of a small cottage and asked for some food.

Merlin looked so hungry and poor that the farmer and his wife took pity on him. They not only gave him a bowl of milk with some brown bread, but they said he might stay through the night.

Merlin saw that, in spite of their pleasant cottage, both the farmer and his wife were very sad.

"Why are you sad?" asked Merlin. "You seem to have a good farm, a pleasant cottage, and many things to make you happy."

"Ah!" said the woman, "we are unhappy because we have no child. I should be the happiest woman in the world if I had a son. Why, even if he were no bigger than my husband's thumb, we should love him dearly."

"That would be indeed a very strange kind of child," said Merlin, "but I hope you may have your wish."

Now Merlin was on his way to call on the queen of the fairies. When he came to her castle the next day, he told the fairy queen the wish of the farmer's wife. The queen of the fairies said, "The good woman shall have her wish. I will give her a son no larger than her husband's thumb."

Soon after this, the good farmer's wife had a son. He was, indeed, just the size of his father's thumb. People came from far and wide to see the tiny boy.

One day the fairy queen and some other fairies came to see him. The queen kissed the little boy and named him Tom Thumb. Each of the other fairies made Tom a gift.

He had a shirt made of silk from a spider's web, a coat of thistledown, a hat made from the leaf of an oak, tiny shoes made from a mouse's skin, and many other gifts besides.

Tom never grew any larger than a man's thumb, but he could do many clever tricks.

One day his mother was mixing a pudding. Tom leaned over the edge of the bowl to see how it was made. He slipped, and in he went, head first.

His mother did not see him fall, and kept stirring and stirring the pudding.

Tom could not see nor hear, but he kicked and kicked inside the pudding.

The pudding moved and tossed about. His mother was afraid. She did not know what to think.

"There must be witches in it," she said.

She went to the window to throw the pudding out. Just then, a poor beggar was passing by the house.

"Here is a pudding you may have, if you like," said Tom's mother.

The beggar thanked her and put it into his basket. He had not gone very far, when Tom got his head out of the pudding and shouted in a shrill voice: "Take me out! take me out!"

The poor beggar was so frightened that he dropped his basket, pudding and all, and ran off as fast as he could.

Tom crawled out of the pudding, climbed out of the basket, and ran home. His mother washed him and put him to bed.

Not long after this Tom's mother took him with her when she went to milk the cow. That he might not get lost, she tied him to a wisp of hay.

When Tom's mother was not looking, the cow took the wisp of hay into her mouth. She began to chew and chew.

Tom began to jump about and shout. He frightened the cow so that she opened her great mouth and out Tom jumped.

Then Tom's mother took him in her apron and ran with him to the house, but he was not hurt in the least.

One day Tom was in the field helping his father. "Let me drive the horse home," said Tom "You drive the horse!" said his father.

"How could you hold the reins?"

"I could stand in the horse's ear and tell him which way to go," said Tom.

So his father put him in the horse's ear, and he drove safely home.

"Mother! mother!" cried Tom.

But when Tom's mother came out, she could see no one. She began to be afraid.

"Where are you, Tom?" she cried.

"Here I am in the horse's ear. Please take me down," said Tom.

His mother lifted him gently down, kissed him, and gave him a blackberry for his supper.

Tom's father made him a whip out of a straw.

Tom tried to drive the cows, but he fell into a deep ditch. There a great bird saw him and thought he was a mouse. The bird seized Tom in her claws and carried him toward her nest.

As they were passing over the sea, Tom got away and fell into the water, where a great fish swallowed him at one mouthful. Soon after this the fish was caught, and it was such a big one that it was sent at once to King Arthur.

When the cook cut open the fish, out jumped Tom Thumb. Tom was brought before the king, and his story was told.

The king grew very fond of Tom and his wise sayings. He took Tom with him wherever he went.

If it began to rain, Tom would creep into the king's pocket and sleep until the rain was over.

The king had a new suit made for Tom, and gave him a needle for a sword. A mouse was trained for Tom to ride. The king and queen never tired of seeing him ride his queer little horse and bravely wave his sword.

One day, as they were going hunting, a cat jumped out and caught Tom's mouse.

Tom drew his sword and tried to drive the cat away.

The king ran to help poor Tom, but the little mouse was dead, and Tom was scratched and bitten. Tom was put to bed, but he did not die. No indeed! He was soon well again, and fought many brave battles and did many brave deeds to please the king.

Written Summation

Model Practice 1

Tom leaned over the edge of the bowl to see how it was made. He slipped, and in he went, head first.

Tom crawled out of the pudding, climbed out of the basket, and ran home. His mother washed him and put him to bed.

Model Practice 2

Model Practice 3

CHAPTER III

Poetry from or about Medieval History

Note: Poetry models should be written in the same manner that the author wrote them, meaning indentions and punctuation.

Each line of poetry should begin on a new line. If the student cannot fit the line of the model on one line, he should continue the sentence on the next line with an indention at the beginning.

For an example, see the model to "Rex Arthurus" on page III-16.

Aladdin
from The Ontario Readers: Fourth Book
by Lowell

When I was a beggarly boy
And lived in a cellar damp,
I had not a friend or a toy,
But I had Aladdin's lamp;
When I could not sleep for cold,
I had fire enough in my brain,
And builded with roofs of gold
My beautiful castles in Spain!

Since then I have toiled day and night,
I have money and power good store,
But I'd give all my lamps of silver bright
For the one that is mine no more;
Take, Fortune, whatever you choose,
You gave, and may snatch again;
I have nothing 'twould pain me to lose,
For I own no more castles in Spain!

Model Practice 1

I had not a friend or a toy,

But I had Aladdin's lamp.

But I'd give all my lamps of silver
    bright
For the one that is mine no more;

Model Practice 2

Model Practice 3

Baa, Baa, Black Sheep
<u>Ring O' Roses A Nursery Rhyme Picture Book</u>
by Anonymous

Baa, baa, Black Sheep,
  Have you any wool?
Yes, marry, have I,
  Three bags full:

One for my master,
  And one for my Dame,
And one for the little boy
  That lives in the lane!

Model Practice 1

Baa, baa, Black Sheep,

Have you any wool?

Yes, marry, have I,

Three bags full.

One for my master,
   And one for my Dame,
And one for the little boy
   That lives in the lane!

Model Practice 2

Model Practice 3

Cock-A-Doodle-Doo
Ring O' Roses A Nursery Rhyme Picture Book
by Anonymous

Cock-a-doodle-doo!
My dame has lost her shoe;
My master's lost his fiddling-stick,
And don't know what to do.

Cock-a-doodle-doo!
What is my dame to do?
Till master finds his fiddling-stick,
She'll dance without her shoe.

Cock-a-doodle-doo!
My dame has lost her shoe,
And master's found his fiddling-stick;
Sing doodle-doodle-doo!

Cock-a-doodle-doo!
My dame will dance with you,
While master fiddles his fiddling-stick,
For dame and doodle-doo.

Cock-a-doodle-doo!
Dame has lost her shoe;
Gone to bed and scratched her head,
And can't tell what to do.

Model Practice 1

Cock-a-doodle-doo!

What is my dame to do?

Till master finds his

fiddling-stick,

She'll dance without

her shoe.

Cock-a-doodle-doo!
Dame has lost her shoe;
Gone to bed and scratched her head,
And can't tell what to do.

Model Practice 2

Model Practice 3

Columbus
1451 - 1506
by Joaquin Miller

Behind him lay the gray Azores,
    Behind the gates of Hercules;
Before him not the ghost of shores,
    Before him only shoreless seas.
The good mate said: "Now must we pray,
    For lo! the very stars are gone;
Speak, Admiral, what shall I say?"
    "Why say, sail on! and on!"

"My men grow mut'nous day by day;
    My men grow ghastly wan and weak."
The stout mate thought of home; a spray
    Of salt wave wash'd his swarthy cheek.
"What shall I say, brave Admiral,
    If we sight naught but seas at dawn?"
"Why, you shall say, at break of day:
    'Sail on! sail on! and on!'"

They sailed and sailed, as winds might blow,
    Until at last the blanch'd mate said;
"Why, now, not even God would know
    Should I and all my men fall dead.
These very winds forget their way,
    For God from these dread seas is gone.
Now speak, brave Admiral, and say——"
    He said: "Sail on! and on!"

They sailed, they sailed, then spoke his mate:
    "This mad sea shows his teeth tonight,
He curls his lip, he lies in wait,
    With lifted teeth as if to bite!
Brave Admiral, say but one word;
    What shall we do when hope is gone?"
The words leaped as a leaping sword:
    "Sail on! sail on! and on!"

Then, pale and worn, he kept his deck,
    And thro' the darkness peered that night.
Ah, darkest night! and then a speck,—
    A light! a light! a light! a light!
It grew—a star-lit flag unfurled!
    It grew to be Time's burst of dawn;
He gained a world! he gave that world
    Its watch-word: "On! and on!"

Model Practice 1

Brave Admiral, say but

one word;

What shall we do when

hope is gone?

The words leaped as a leaping sword: " Sail on! Sail on! And on! "

Model Practice 2

Model Practice 3

Rex Arthurus
from The Classic Mother Goose
by Jacob Bigelow

When King Arthur ruled the land,
He ruled it like a king:
He bought four pecks of barley-meal
To make a brave pudding.

A pudding brave the king did make
And stuffed it well with plums;
Great lumps of suet he put into it,
As big as both his thumbs.

The king and queen partook thereof,
And all the court beside;
And what they did not eat that night,
The queen next morning fried.

Model Practice 1

When King Arthur ruled

the land,

He ruled it like a king.

The king and queen partook thereof,
And all the court beside;
And what they did not eat that night,
The queen next morning fried.

Model Practice 2

Model Practice 3

The Greenwood Tree
from The Ontario Readers: Fourth Book
by Shakespeare

      Under the greenwood tree
      Who loves to lie with me,
      And tune his merry note
      Unto the sweet bird's throat,
Come hither, come hither, come hither;
      Here shall he see
      No enemy
But winter and rough weather.

      Who doth ambition shun
      And loves to live i' the sun;
      Seeking the food he eats,
      And pleased with what he gets,
Come hither, come hither, come hither;
      Here shall he see
      No enemy
But winter and rough weather.

Model Practice 1

Under the greenwood tree

Who loves to lie with me,

And tune his merry note

Unto the sweet bird's

throat,

Who doth ambition shun
And loves to live i' the sun;
Seeking the food he eats,
And pleased with what he gets,

Model Practice 2

Model Practice 3

Ingratitude
from <u>Poems Every Child Should Know</u>
by William Shakespeare

"Ingratitude," by William Shakespeare (1564-1616), is an incisive thrust at a refined vice. It is a part of education to learn to be grateful.

Blow, blow, thou winter wind,
Thou are not so unkind
As man's ingratitude;
Thy tooth is not so keen
Because thou are not seen,
Although thy breath be rude.
Freeze, freeze, thou bitter sky,
Thou dost not bite so nigh
As benefits forgot;
Though thou the waters warp,
Thy sting is not so sharp
As friend remembered not.

Model Practice 1

Blow, blow, thou winter

wind,

Thou are not so unkind

As man's ingratitude;

Thy tooth is not so keen
Because thou are not seen,
Although thy breath be rude.

Model Practice 2

Model Practice 3

I Saw a Ship A-Sailing
from The Real Mother Goose
by Unknown

I saw a ship a-sailing,
A-sailing on the sea;
And, oh, it was all laden
With pretty things for thee!

There were comfits in the cabin,
And apples in the hold;
The sails were made of silk,
And the masts were made of gold.

The four and twenty sailors
That stood between the decks
Were four and twenty white mice,
With chains about their necks.

The captain was a duck,
With a jacket on his back;
And when the ship began to move,
The captain said, "Quack! quack!"

Model Practice 1

The sails were made of,

silk,

And the masts were made

of gold.

The four and twenty sailors
That stood between the decks
Were four and twenty white mice,
With chains about their necks.

Model Practice 2

Model Practice 3

Saint Bernard's Hymn

1091-1153
from the Library Of The World's Best Literature, Ancient And Modern, Vol 4
collected by Charles Dudley Warner

    Jesu! the very thought of thee
      With sweetness fills my breast,
    But sweeter far thy face to see
      And in thy presence rest.

    Nor voice can sing nor heart can frame,
      Nor can the memory find,
    A sweeter sound than thy blest name,
      O Savior of mankind!

    O hope of every contrite heart!
      O joy of all the meek!
    To those who fall, how kind thou art,
      How good to those who seek!

    But what to those who find? Ah, this
      Nor tongue nor pen can show.
    The love of Jesus, what it is
      None but his loved ones know.

    Jesu! our only joy be thou,
      As thou our prize wilt be!
    Jesu! be thou our glory now
      And through eternity!

Model Practice 1

O hope of every contrite

heart!

O joy of all the meek!

To those who fall, how kind thou art,
How good to those who seek!

Model Practice 2

Model Practice 3

The Sermon of St. Francis
1182 - 1226
from the De La Salle Series
by Henry Wadsworth Longfellow

    Up soared the lark into the air,
    A shaft of song, a wingèd prayer,
    As if a soul, released from pain,
    Were flying back to heaven again.

    St. Francis heard; it was to him
    An emblem of the Seraphim;
    The upward motion of the fire,
    The light, the heat, the heart's desire.

    Around Assisi's convent gate
    The birds, God's poor who cannot wait,
    From moor and mere and darksome wood
    Came flocking for their dole of food.

    "O brother birds," St. Francis said,
    "Ye come to me and ask for bread,
    But not with bread alone to-day
    Shall ye be fed and sent away.

    "Ye shall be fed, ye happy birds
    With manna of celestial words;
    Not mine, though mine they seem to be,
    Not mine, though they be spoken through me.

    "O, doubly are ye bound to praise
    The great Creator in your lays;
    He giveth you your plumes of down,
    Your crimson hoods, your cloaks of brown.

    "He giveth you your wings to fly
    And breathe a purer air on high,
    And careth for you everywhere,
    Who for yourselves so little care!"

    With flutter of swift wings and songs
    Together rose the feathered throngs,
    And singing scattered far apart;
    Deep peace was in St. Francis' heart.

    He knew not if the brotherhood
    His homily had understood;
    He only knew that to one ear
    The meaning of his words was clear.

Model Practice 1

"O brother birds," St.

Francis said,

"Ye come to me and ask

for bread,"

But not with bread alone to-day
Shall ye be fed and sent away.

Model Practice 2

Model Practice 3

To Market To Market
from Ring O' Roses A Nursery Rhyme Picture Book
by Anonymous

To market, to market, to buy a fat Pig;
Home again, home again, dancing a jig.

To market, to market, to buy a fat Hog;
Home again, home again, jiggety-jog.

Model Practice 1

To market, to market, to

buy a fat Pig;

Home again, home again,

dancing a jig.

To market, to market, to buy a
    fat Hog;
Home again, home again, jiggety-jog.

Model Practice 2

Model Practice 3

CHAPTER IV

Tales from Various Cultures

The Frog's Travels
from a <u>Story Hour Reader</u>
by Ida Coe and Alice J. Christie
Japanese Tale

Long, long ago, in the country of Japan, there were two frogs. One of the frogs lived in a pond near Tokyo. And the other lived in a little stream near Kyoto.

One fine morning in early spring, these two frogs decided that they would travel forth to see the world.

Strangely enough, though they had never heard of each other, the same thought came to each frog at the same time.

The first frog started along the road which led from Tokyo to Kyoto.

He found the journey difficult and the road hard to travel. So when he had hopped to the top of a high hill halfway, he decided to stop a while and rest.

The other frog started out on the same road, but from Kyoto. It took him a long time to reach the hill where the first frog was resting.

The two frogs met at the top of the hill. They were delighted to make each other's acquaintance.

"Greetings, friend!" said the first of the two frogs. "Where are you going?"

"I have a great desire to see the world, and especially to visit Tokyo. I am on my way for a visit to Tokyo now," replied the second frog.

"There is no need of hurrying. Let us rest here and stretch our limbs," said the first frog.

"What a pity that we are not taller!" said the Kyoto frog.

"Why?" asked the Tokyo frog.

"If we were taller, we could see both towns from this hill. Then we should be able to tell whether or not it were worthwhile to continue our journey," said the Kyoto frog.

"Oh, we can easily find that out!" replied the other.

"We can stand on our hind legs and take hold of one another. Then each can look at the town toward which he is traveling," he added.

"A fine idea! Let us try it at once."

The two frogs stood upon their hind legs, holding each other tightly to keep from falling.

The Tokyo frog turned toward Kyoto, and the Kyoto frog turned toward Tokyo.

The foolish frogs forgot that their eyes were on the backs of their heads.

Although their noses pointed toward the places they wished to go, their eyes beheld the towns from which they had just come.

"Indeed, I shall travel no further!" the first frog exclaimed.

"Kyoto is exactly like Tokyo. I shall go home at once," he added.

"Tokyo is only a copy of Kyoto," said the other frog.

"It is not worth while to take the trouble to journey there!" he added disdainfully.

The two frogs bade each other a polite farewell, and each returned to his own hometown. To the end of their lives, the two frogs believed that Tokyo and Kyoto were really exactly alike. Neither of the frogs ever again tried to see the world.

Written Summation

Model Practice 1

One of the frogs lived

in a pond near Tokyo.

And the other lived in

a little stream near

Kyoto.

"What a pity that we are not taller!" said the Kyoto frog.
"Why?" asked the Tokyo frog.

Model Practice 2

Model Practice 3

How Indian Corn Came into the World

from Good Stories for Great Holidays
an Ojibbeway Legend
adapted by Henry R. Schoolcraft

(Note: Parents pre-read for violence.)

Long, long ago, in a beautiful part of this country, there lived an Indian with his wife and children. He was poor and found it hard to provide food enough for his family. But though needy, he was kind and contented and always gave thanks to the Great Spirit for everything that he received. His eldest son, Wunzh, was likewise kind and gentle and thankful of heart. He too longed greatly to do something for his people.

The time came that Wunzh reached the age when every Indian boy fasts so that he may see in a vision the Spirit that is to be his guide through life. Wunzh's father built him a little lodge apart, so that the boy might rest there undisturbed during his days of fasting. Then Wunzh withdrew to begin the solemn rite.

On the first day, he walked alone in the woods looking at the flowers and plants. He filled his mind with the beautiful images of growing things so that he might see them in his night dreams. He saw how the flowers, herbs, and berries grew. He knew that some were good for food and that others healed wounds and cured sickness. And his heart was filled with an even greater longing to do something for his family and his tribe.

"Truly," thought he, "the Great Spirit made all things. To Him we owe our lives. But could He not make it easier for us to get our food than by hunting and catching fish? I must try to find this out in my vision."

So Wunzh returned to his lodge and fasted and slept. On the third day, he became weak and faint. Soon he saw in a vision a young brave coming down from the sky and approaching the lodge. He was clad in rich garments of green and yellow colors. On his head was a tuft of nodding green plumes, and all his motions were graceful and swaying.

"I am sent to you, O Wunzh," said the sky-stranger, "by that Great Spirit who made all things in sky and earth. He has seen your fasting, and knows how you wish to do good to your people, and that you do not seek for strength in war nor for the praise of warriors. I am sent to tell you how you may do good to your kindred. Arise and wrestle with me, for only by overcoming me may you learn the secret."

Wunzh, though he was weak from fasting, felt courage grow in his heart. He arose and wrestled with the stranger. But soon he became weaker and exhausted, and the stranger, seeing this, smiled gently on him and said: "My friend, this is enough for once, I will come again tomorrow." And he vanished as suddenly as he had appeared.

The next day the stranger came, and Wunzh felt himself weaker than before; nevertheless, he rose and wrestled bravely. Then the stranger spoke a second time. "My friend," he said, "have courage! Tomorrow will be your last trial." And he disappeared from Wunzh's sight.

On the third day, the stranger came as before, and the struggle was renewed. And Wunzh, though fainter in body, grew strong in mind and will, and he determined to win or perish in the attempt. He exerted all his powers. And, lo, in a while, he prevailed and overcame the stranger.

"O Wunzh, my friend," said the conquered one, "you have wrestled manfully. You have met your trial well. Tomorrow I shall come again and you must wrestle with me for the last time. You will prevail. Then you must strip off my garments, throw me down, clean the earth of roots and weeds, and bury me in that spot. When you have done so, leave my body in the ground. Come often to the place and see whether I have come to life, but be careful not to let weeds or grass grow on my grave. If you do all this well, you will soon discover how to benefit your fellow creatures." Having said this the stranger disappeared.

In the morning, Wunzh's father came to him with food. "My son," he said, "you have fasted long. It is seven days since you have tasted food, and you must not sacrifice your life. The Master of Life does not require that."

"My father," replied the boy, "wait until the sun goes down tomorrow. For a certain reason I wish to fast until that hour."

"Very well," said the old man, "I shall wait until the time arrives when you feel inclined to eat." And he went away.

The next day, at the usual hour, the sky stranger came again. And, though Wunzh had fasted seven days, he felt a new power arise within him. He grasped the stranger with superhuman strength and threw him down. He took from him his beautiful garments, and, finding him dead, buried him in the softened earth and did all else as he had been directed.

He then returned to his father's lodge and partook sparingly of food. There he abode for some time. But he never forgot the grave of his friend. Daily he visited it and pulled up the weeds and grass and kept the earth soft and moist. Very soon, to his great wonder, he saw the tops of green plumes coming through the ground.

Weeks passed by, the summer was drawing to a close. One day Wunzh asked his father to follow him. He led him to a distant meadow. There, in the place where the stranger had been buried, stood a tall and graceful plant with bright-colored, silken hair, and crowned by nodding green plumes. Its stalk was covered with waving leaves. And there grew from its sides clusters of milk-filled ears of corn, golden and sweet, each ear closely wrapped in its green husks.

"It is my friend!" shouted the boy joyously; "it is Mondawmin, the Indian Corn! We need no longer depend on hunting, so long as this gift is planted and cared for. The Great Spirit has heard my voice and has sent us this food."

Then the whole family feasted on the ears of corn and thanked the Great Spirit who gave it. So Indian Corn came into the world.

Written Summation

Model Practice 1

So Wunzh returned
to his lodge and fasted
and slept. On the third
day, he became weak
and faint.

He then returned to his father's lodge and partook sparingly of food. There he abode for some time.

Model Practice 2

Model Practice 3

The Necklace of Truth
from the Book of Stories for The Story-Teller
by Jean Mace

Once there was a little girl named Coralie. She had but one fault. She told falsehoods. Her parents tried to cure her in many ways, but in vain. Finally, they decided to take her to the enchanter Merlin.

The enchanter Merlin lived in a glass palace. He loved truth. He knew liars by their odor a league off. When Coralie came toward the castle, Merlin was forced to burn vinegar to keep himself from being ill.

Coralie's mother began to explain the reason for their coming. But Merlin stopped her.

"I know all about your daughter, my good lady," he said. "She is one of the greatest liars in the world. She often makes me ill."

Merlin's face looked so stern that Coralie hid her face under her mother's cloak. Her father stood before her to keep her from harm.

"Do not fear," said Merlin. "I am not going to hurt your little girl. I only wish to make her a present."

He opened a drawer and took from it a magnificent amethyst necklace. It was fastened with a shining clasp of diamonds.

Merlin put the necklace on Coralie's neck and said, "Go in peace, my friends. Your little daughter carries with her a sure guardian of the truth."

Then he looked sternly at Coralie and said, "In a year I shall come for my necklace. Do not dare to take it off for a single moment. If you do, harm will come to you!"

"Oh, I shall always love to wear it! It is so beautiful!" cried Coralie. And this is the way she came by the wonderful Necklace of Truth.

The day after Coralie returned home she was sent to school. As she had long been absent, the little girls crowded round her. There was a cry of admiration at sight of the necklace.

"Where did it come from? Where did you get it?" they asked.

"I was ill for a long time," replied Coralie. "When I got well, mamma and papa gave me the necklace."

A loud cry rose from all. The diamonds of the clasp had grown dim. They now looked like coarse glass.

"Yes, indeed, I have been ill! What are you making such a fuss about?"

At this second falsehood, the amethysts changed to ugly yellow stones. A new cry arose. Coralie was frightened at the strange behavior of the necklace.

"I have been to the enchanter Merlin," she said very humbly.

Immediately the necklace looked as beautiful as ever. But the children teased her.

"You need not laugh," said Coralie, "for Merlin was very glad to see us. He sent his carriage to the next town to meet us. Such a splendid carriage, with six white horses, pink satin cushions, and a coachman with powdered hair. Merlin's palace is all of jasper and gold. He met us at the door and led us to the dining room. There stood a long table covered with delicious things to eat. First of all we ate——"

Coralie stopped, for the children were laughing till the tears rolled down their cheeks. She glanced at the necklace and shuddered. With each new falsehood, the necklace had become longer and longer, till it already dragged on the ground.

"Coralie, you are stretching the truth," cried the girls.

"Well, I confess it. We walked, and we stayed there only five minutes."

The necklace shrank at once to its proper size.

"The necklace—the necklace—where did it come from?"

"He gave it to me without saying a word. I think——"

She had not time to finish. The fatal necklace grew shorter and shorter till it choked her. She gasped for breath.

"You are keeping back part of the truth," cried her schoolmates.

"He said—that I was—one of the greatest—liars in the world." The necklace loosened about her neck, but Coralie still cried with pain.

"That was why Merlin gave me the necklace. He said that it would make me truthful. What a silly I have been to be proud of it!"

Her playmates were sorry for her. "If I were in your place," said one of them, "I should send back the necklace. Why do you not take it off?"

Poor Coralie did not wish to speak. The stones, however, began to dance up and down and to make a terrible clatter.

"There is something you have not told us," laughed the little girls.

"I like to wear it."

Oh, how the diamonds and amethysts danced! It was worse than ever.

"Tell us the true reason."

"Well, I see I can hide nothing. Merlin forbade me to take it off. He said great harm would come if I disobeyed."

Thanks to the enchanted necklace, Coralie became a truthful child. Long before the year had passed, Merlin came for his necklace. He needed it for another child who told falsehoods.

No one can tell today what has become of the wonderful Necklace of Truth. But if I were a little child in the habit of telling falsehoods, I should not feel quite sure that it might not be found again some fine day.

Written Summation

Model Practice 1

"I was ill for a long time," replied Coralie. "When I got well, mamma and papa gave me the necklace."

Poor Coralie did not wish to speak. The stones, however, began to dance up and down and to make a terrible clatter.

Model Practice 2

Model Practice 3

The Pancake
from East O' the Sun and West O' the Moon
by Gudrun Thorne-Thomsen

Once on a time there was a woman who had seven hungry children, and she was frying a pancake for them. It was a sweet milk pancake, and there it lay in the pan, bubbling and frizzling so thick and good, it was a delight to look at it. And the children stood round about, and the old father sat by and looked on.

"Oh, give me a bit of pancake, mother, dear, I am so hungry," said one child.

"Oh, darling mother," said the second.

"Oh, darling, good mother," said the third.

"Oh, darling, good, sweet mother," said the fourth.

"Oh, darling, pretty, good, sweet mother," said the fifth.

"Oh, darling, pretty, good, sweet, clever mother," said the sixth.

"Oh, darling, pretty, good, sweet, clever, kindest little mother," said the seventh.

So they begged for the pancake all around, the one more prettily than the other, for they were so hungry and so good.

"Yes, yes, children, only bide a bit till it turns itself and then you shall have some lovely sweet milk pancake. Only look how fat and happy it lies there."

But she ought to have said, 'till I can get it turned,' because when the pancake heard all this it became afraid, and in a trice it turned itself and tried to jump out of the pan, but it fell back into it again, the other side up. When it had been fried a little on the other side too, till it got firm and stiff, it jumped out of the pan to the floor and rolled off like a wheel through the door and down the hill.

"Holloa! Stop, pancake!" and away ran the mother after it, with the frying pan in one hand and the ladle in the other, as fast as she could, and all the children behind her, while the old father on crutches limped after them last of all.

"Hi! Won't you stop? Catch it! Stop, pancake!" they all screamed out, one after another, and tried to catch it on the run and hold it. But the pancake rolled on and on, and in a twinkling of an eye, it was so far ahead that they couldn't see it.

So when it had rolled awhile it met a man.

"Good-day, pancake," said the man.

"Good-day, Manny Panny!" said the pancake.

"Dear pancake," said the man, "don't roll so fast. Stop a little and let me eat you."

"No, no; I have run away from the mother, and the father, and seven hungry children. I'll run away from you, Manny Panny," said the pancake, and it rolled and rolled till it met a hen.

"Good-day, pancake," said the hen.

"The same to you, Henny Penny," said the pancake.

"Pancake, dear, don't roll so fast. Bide a bit and let me eat you up," said the hen.

"No, no; I have run away from the mother, and the father, and seven hungry children, and Manny Panny. I'll run away from you, too, Henny Penny," said the pancake, and it rolled on like a wheel down the road.

Just then, it met a cock.

"Good-day, pancake," said the cock.

"The same to you, Cocky Locky," said the pancake.

"Pancake, dear, don't roll so fast, but bide a bit and let me eat you up."

"No, no; I have run away from the mother, and the father, seven hungry children, Manny Panny, and Henny Penny. I'll run away from you too, Cocky Locky," said the pancake, and it rolled and rolled as fast as it could. Bye and bye, it met a duck.

"Good-day, pancake," said the duck.

"The same to you, Ducky Lucky."

"Pancake, dear, don't roll away so fast; bide a bit and let me eat you up."

"No, no; I have run away from the mother, and the father, and seven hungry children, Manny Panny, Henny Penny, and Cocky Locky. I'll run away from you, too, Ducky Lucky," said the pancake, and with that, it took to rolling and rolling faster than ever; and when it had rolled a long, long while, it met a goose.

"Good-day, pancake," said the goose.

"The same to you, Goosey Loosey."

"Pancake, dear, don't roll so fast. Bide a bit and let me eat you up."

"No, no; I have run away from the mother, the father, seven hungry children, Manny Panny, Henny Penny, Cocky Locky, and Ducky Lucky. I'll run away from you, too, Goosey Loosey," said the pancake, and off it rolled.

So when it had rolled a long way off, it met a gander.

"Good-day, pancake," said the gander.

"The same to you, Gander Pander," said the pancake.

"Pancake, dear, don't roll so fast; bide a bit and let me have a bite."

"No, no; I've run away from the mother, the father, seven hungry children, Manny Panny, Henny Penny, Cocky Locky, Ducky Lucky, and Goosey Loosey. I'll run away from you, too, Gander Pander," said the pancake, and it rolled and rolled as fast as ever.

So when it had rolled a long, long time, it met a pig.

"Good-day, pancake," said the pig.

"The same to you, Piggy Wiggy," said the pancake, and without a word more, it began to roll and roll for dear life.

"Nay, nay," said the pig, "you needn't be in such a hurry; we two can go side by side through the wood; they say it is not too safe in there."

The pancake thought there might be something in that, and so they kept company. But when they had gone a while, they came to a brook. As for Piggy, he was so fat he could swim across. It was nothing for him, but the poor pancake could not get over.

"Seat yourself on my snout," said the pig, "and I'll carry you over."

So the pancake did that.

"Ouf, ouf," said the pig, and swallowed the pancake at one gulp, and then, as the poor pancake could go no farther, why—this story can go no farther either.

Written Summation

Model Practice 1

So when it had rolled

awhile it met a man.

"Good-day, pancake,"

said the man.

"Pancake, dear, don't roll so fast. Bide a bit and let me eat you up," said the hen.

Model Practice 2

Model Practice 3

Tale of a Dumb Witness
from a <u>Child's World Reader</u>
by Hetty Browne, Sarah Withers, W.K. Tate
Arabian Tale

One day at noontime, a poor man was riding along a road. He was tired and hungry and wished to stop and rest. Finding a tree with low branches, he tied his horse to one of them. Then he sat down to eat his dinner.

Soon a rich man came along and started to tie his horse to the same tree.

"Do not fasten your horse to that tree," cried the poor man. "My horse is savage, and he may kill yours. Fasten him to another tree."

"I shall tie my horse where I wish," the rich man replied; and he tied his horse to the same tree. Then he, too, sat down to eat.

Very soon, the men heard a great noise. They looked up and saw that their horses were kicking and fighting. Both men rushed to stop them, but it was too late; the rich man's horse was dead.

"See what your horse has done!" cried the rich man in an angry voice. "But you shall pay for it! You shall pay for it!"

Then he dragged the man before a judge.

"Oh, wise judge," he cried, "I have come to you for justice. I had a beautiful, kind, gentle horse which has been killed by this man's savage horse. Make the man pay for the horse or send him to prison."

"Not so fast, my friend," the judge said. "There are two sides to every case."

The judge turned to the poor man. "Did your horse kill this man's horse?" he asked.

The poor man made no reply.

The judge asked in surprise, "Are you dumb? Can you not talk?"

But no word came from the poor man's lips.

Then the judge turned to the rich man. "What more can I do?" he asked. "You see for yourself this poor man cannot speak."

"Oh, but he can," cried the rich man. "He spoke to me."

"Indeed!" said the judge. "When?"

"He spoke to me when I tied my horse to the tree."

"What did he say?" asked the judge.

"He said, 'Do not fasten your horse to that tree. My horse is savage and may kill yours.'"

"O ho!" said the judge. "This poor man warned you that his horse was savage, and you tied your horse near his after the warning. This puts a new light on the matter. You are to blame, not he."

The judge turned to the poor man and said, "My man, why did you not answer my questions?"

"Oh, wise judge," said the poor man, "if I had told you that I warned him not to tie his horse near mine, he would have denied it. Then how could you have told which one of us to believe? I let him tell his own story, and you have learned the truth."

This speech pleased the judge. He praised the poor man for his wisdom and sent the rich man away without a penny.

Written Summation

Model Practice 1

Finding a tree with low branches, he tied his horse to one of them. Then he sat down to eat his dinner.

"See what your horse has done!" cried the rich man in an angry voice. "But you shall pay for it! You shall pay for it!"

Model Practice 2

Model Practice 3

The Three Billy Goats Gruff
from East O' the Sun and West O' the Moon
by Gudrun Thorne-Thomsen

Once on a time there were three Billy Goats, who were to go up to the hillside to make themselves fat. The family name of the goats was "Gruff."

On the way up was a bridge over a river which they had to cross, and under the bridge lived a great ugly Troll with eyes as big as saucers and a nose as long as a poker.

First of all came the youngest Billy Goat Gruff to cross the bridge. "Trip, trap; trip, trap!" went the bridge.

"*Who's that tripping over my bridge?*" roared the Troll.

"Oh, it is only I, the tiniest Billy Goat Gruff, and I'm going up to the hillside to make myself fat," said the Billy Goat, with such a small voice.

"Now, I'm coming to gobble you up," said the Troll.

"Oh, no! Pray do not take me. I'm too little, that I am," said the Billy Goat. "Wait a bit till the second Billy Goat Gruff comes. He's much bigger."

"Well! Be off with you," said the Troll.

A little while after came the second Billy Goat Gruff across the bridge.

"Trip, trap! Trip, trap! Trip, trap!" went the bridge.

"*Who is that tripping over my bridge?*" roared the Troll.

"Oh, it's the second Billy Goat Gruff, and I'm going up to the hillside to make myself fat," said the Billy Goat. Nor had he such a small voice, either.

"Now, I'm coming to gobble you up!" said the Troll.

"Oh, no! Don't take me, wait a little till the big Billy Goat comes, he's much bigger."

"Very well! Be off with you," said the Troll.

But just then up came the big Billy Goat Gruff.

"Trip, trap! Trip, trap! Trip, trap!" went the bridge. For the Billy Goat was so heavy that the bridge creaked and groaned under him.

"*Who's that tramping on my bridge?*" roared the Troll.

"It's I! The big Billy Goat Gruff," said the Billy Goat, and he had a big hoarse voice.

"Now, I'm coming to gobble you up!" roared the troll.

"Well come! I have two spears so stout,
With them I'll thrust your eyeballs out;
I have besides two great big stones,
With them I'll crush you body and bones!"

That was what the big Billy Goat said; so he flew at the Troll, and thrust him with his horns, and crushed him to bits, body and bones, and tossed him out into the river, and after that he went up to the hillside.

There the Billy Goats got so fat that they were scarcely able to walk home again, and if they haven't grown thinner, why they're still fat; and so, —

"Snip, snap, stout.
This tale's told out."

Written Summation

Model Practice 1

First of all came the youngest Billy Goat Gruff to cross the bridge.

"Trip trap! Trip trap!" went the bridge.

"Trip, trap! Trip, trap!" went the bridge. For the Billy Goat was so heavy that the bridge creaked and groaned under him.

Model Practice 2

Model Practice 3

Why the Bear's Tail Is Short
from a Beacon Second Reader
by James H. Fassett
German Folktale

Did you ever go to a circus where there was a bear in a cage? Did you notice how short his tail was? I will tell you how the bear's tail came to be short.

One very cold day in winter, a fox saw some men taking home a load of fish.

The fox jumped upon the wagon while the men were not looking. He threw off some of the best fish until he had enough for his dinner. Then Mr. Fox jumped from the wagon and began to eat the fish.

While he was eating the fish, Mr. Bear came along.

"Good morning," said Mr. Bear, "you have had good luck fishing today. Those are very fine fish. How did you catch them?"

"They are fine fish," said Mr. Fox. "If you will go fishing with me tonight, I will show you how to catch even better fish than these."

"I will go with you gladly," said the bear. "I will bring my hook and line too."

"You don't need a hook and line," said the fox.

"I always catch fish with my tail. You have a much longer tail than I, and can fish so much the better."

At sunset, the bear met the fox. They went across the frozen river until they came to a small hole in the ice.

"Now, Mr. Bear," said the fox, "sit down here on the ice and put your tail through the hole. You must keep still for a long while. That is the best way to catch fish.

Wait until a great many fish take hold of your tail. Then pull with all your might."

The bear sat very still for a long time. At last, he began to feel cold, and he moved a little.

"Ow!" he cried, for his tail had begun to freeze in the ice. "Is it not time to pull out the fish?" said the bear.

"No, no!" cried the fox. "Wait until more fish have taken hold of your tail. You are very strong. You can wait a little longer."

So the poor bear waited until it was almost morning.

Just then, some dogs began to bark on the bank of the river. The bear was so afraid that he jumped up quickly and pulled with all his might, but his tail was frozen fast in the ice. He pulled and pulled until at length the tail was broken short off.

Mr. Fox ran away laughing and laughing at the trick he had played upon Mr. Bear.

Bears' tails have been short ever since.

Written Summation

Model Practice 1

He threw off some of

the best fish until he had

enough for his dinner.

Then Mr. Fox jumped

from the wagon and

began to eat the fish.

Mr. Fox ran away laughing at the trick he had played upon Mr. Bear.

Model Practice 2

Model Practice 3

The Wolf and the Seven Young Kids
from a Beacon Reader
by William and Jacob Grimm
German Folktale

There was once an old goat who had seven little kids. She loved them all as much as any mother ever loved her children.

One day the old goat wished to go into the woods to get food for her kids. Before she started, she called them all to her and said:

"Dear children, I am going into the woods. Now do not open the door while I am away. If the old wolf should get into our hut, he would eat you all up, and not a hair would be left. You can easily tell him by his rough voice and his black feet."

"Dear mother," cried all the young kids, "we will be very careful not to let the old wolf in. You need not think of us at all, for we shall be quite safe."

So the old goat went on her way into the dark woods.

She had not been gone long when there came a loud rap at the door, and a voice cried, "Open the door, my dear children. I have something here for each of you."

But the young kids knew by the rough voice that this was the old wolf. So one of them said, "We shall not open the door. Our mother's voice is soft and gentle. Your voice is rough. You are a wolf."

The old wolf ran away to a shop, where he ate a piece of white chalk to make his voice soft. Then he went back to the goat's hut and rapped at the door.

He spoke in a soft voice and said, "Open the door for me, my dear children. I am your mother."

But the oldest little goat thought of what his mother had said.

"If you are our mother, put your foot on the window sill, that we may see it."

When the wolf had done this, all the little goats cried out, "No, you are not our mother. We shall not open the door. Our mother's feet are white and yours are black. Go away; you are the wolf."

Then the wolf went to the miller's, and said to him, "Mr. Miller, put some flour on my foot, for I have hurt it."

The miller was so afraid of the wolf that he did as he was told.

Then the wicked wolf went to the goat's house again and said, "Open the door, dear children, for I am your mother."

"Show us your foot," said the little kids.

So the wolf put his one white foot on the windowsill.

When the little kids saw that it was white, they thought this was really their mother. They opened the door. In jumped the ugly old wolf, and all the little kids ran to hide themselves.

The first hid under the table, the second in the bed, the third in the oven, the fourth in the kitchen, the fifth in the cupboard, the sixth under the washtub, and the seventh, who was the smallest of all, in the tall clock.

The wolf quickly found and gobbled up all but the youngest, who was in the clock. Then the wolf, who felt sleepy, went out and lay down on the green grass. Soon he was fast asleep.

Not long after this, the old goat came home from the woods. Ah, what did she see! The house door was wide open. The tables and chairs were upset. The washtub was broken in pieces, and the bed was tipped over.

"Where are my dear children?" cried the poor goat.

At last, she heard a little voice crying, "Dear mother, here I am in the tall clock."

The old goat helped the little goat out. Soon she learned how the wolf had eaten her dear children. Then she went out of the hut, and there on the grass lay the wolf sound asleep.

As the goat looked at the wicked old wolf, she thought she saw something jumping about inside him.

"Ah," she said, "it may be that my poor children are still alive."

So she sent the little kid into the house for a pair of scissors and a needle and some thread.

She quickly cut a hole in the side of the wicked old wolf. At the first snip of the scissors, one of the kids stuck out his head. As the old goat cut, more and more heads popped out. At last, all six of the kids jumped out upon the grass. They went hopping and skipping about their mother.

Then the old goat said to them, "Go and bring me some large stones from the brook."

The seven little kids ran off to the brook and soon came back with seven large stones. They put these stones inside the wicked old wolf.

The old goat sewed up the wolf's side so gently and quietly that he did not wake up nor move.

When at last the wicked wolf did wake up, the great stones inside him made him feel very heavy. He was thirsty, too. So he walked down to the brook to drink. The stones were so heavy that they tipped him over the edge of the bank into the deep water, and he was drowned.

Written Summation

Model Practice 1

When the little kids saw that it was white, they thought this was really their mother. They opened the door.

When at last the wicked wolf did wake up, the great stones inside him made him feel very heavy. He was thirsty, too.

Model Practice 2

Model Practice 3

APPENDIX

Contains Models

For Teacher Use

(Remove and use for dictating to student)

Oral Narration Questions

(Your student may not need these questions, if he can retell the story easily.)

Questions for Chapter I, historical narratives, or Chapter IV, cultural tales.

1. Who was the main character? (Who is the story about?)
2. What was the character like? (What was he or she like?)
3. Where was the character? (Where did the story happen?)
4. What time was it in the story? Time of day? Time of year?
5. Who else was in the story?
6. Does the main character have an enemy? What is the enemy's name? (Is there a bad guy?) (The enemy may also be self or nature.)
7. Does the main character want something? If not, does the main character have a problem?
8. What does the main character do? What does he say? If there are others, what do they do or say?
9. Why does the character do what he does?
10. What happens to the character as he tries to solve his problem?
11. Does the main character solve his problem? How does he solve his problem?
12. What happens at the end of the story?
13. Is there a moral to the story? If so, what was it?

Questions for Chapter III, poetry.

1. Is the poem about a character, an event, or an idea? (Is the poem about a person, place, or thing?)
2. Does this poem express a feeling of happiness, sadness, anger, excitement, joy, hope, determination, or fear?
3. How does the poem make you feel?
4. Do you think the author of the poem had a message?
5. What do you think the message of the poem is?

Written Summations

(Have your student sum up the story in no more than six sentences—two for each question. Less is best)

1. What happened at the beginning of the story?
2. What happened at the middle of the story?
3. What happened at the end of the story?

Principle of Praise

Encourage, build up, praise, and celebrate your student's successes.

*Let no corrupt communication
proceed out of your mouth, but
that which is good to the use of edifying,
that it may minister grace
unto the hearers*

Using the Grammar Guide

On the following page, I have included a guide to introducing the eight parts of speech and basic punctuation. Complete grammar study with copywork. For some students, especially first graders, teaching only the first few months of material will be enough. **Feel free to focus on the material covered in month one for two months or longer.** Have your student:

1. Read the model.
2. Copy the model.
3. Return to the model and circle the correct parts of speech in the proper colors. See page 4.
4. **For older students only,** have them label the parts of speech according to the definitions below.

Label   Definition

nouns   DO, IO, PN   **direct object, indirect object, or predicate nominative**

Subject is the noun that is or does something. (Who ran? What stinks?)	I ran. **The dog** stinks.
Direct objects answers what. (I ate what?)	I ate **the cookie**.
Indirect objects tell for whom the action of the verb was done.	I gave **her** the cookie.
Predicate Nominative (Noun LinkingVerb Noun.)	John is my **dad**.

verbs   AV, SB, LV   **action verb, state of being, or linking verb**

Action verbs with a direct object are transitive verbs.	(He kicked the ball.)
Action verbs without a direct object are intransitive.	(He kicked.)
State of being verbs are the "to be" verbs.	(am, are, is, was, were, be, being, been)
Helping verbs help the main verb express time and mood.	(do run, can clean, am eating, might hit)
Linking verbs link the subject to the predicate.	(The wind grew chilly. The wind was chilly.)
	(If I can replace grew with was, it is a LV.)

pronouns   SP, OP, PP, DP   **Subject, Object, Possessive, Demonstrative**

Subject Pronouns	I, you, he, she, it, we, they	We love to read. It was outside.
Object Pronouns	me, you, him, her, it, us, them	She took it. I handed them the candy.
Possessive Pronouns	mine, yours, his, hers, theirs, ours, its, whose	That is **mine**! Ours is blue.
Demonstrative Pronouns	this, that, these, those	**That** is mine! We love that.

adjectives   AA, PA, DA   **Attributive, Predicate, or Demonstrative Adjectives**

Attributive Adjectives modify the noun and are right next to it.	(The **big** car.)
Predicate Adjectives follow linking verbs.	(The car is **big**.)
Demonstrative Adjectives (This, that, these, those)	**That** flower grew.

adverbs   where, how, when, extent

Adverbs that tell where, how, and when modify an adverb.	(up, down, quickly, softly, yesterday, now)
Adverbs that tell extent modify an adverb or adjective.	(almost, also, only, very, enough, rather, too)

prepositions   OP   **object of the preposition**

GRAMMAR GUIDE

Optional: At the start of each month place memory work on flashcards

Month 1   Nouns

All	Memorize the definition of a noun below.
	Give your student examples of a noun.
	Have him give you examples.
	Work with your student to identify the nouns in the copywork model.
	Circle the nouns blue.
	Teach your student about capitalization.
Older students	Teach the difference between a common noun and a proper noun.

Nouns   <u>circle blue</u>   **a word that names a person, place, thing, or idea**

    Common nouns   (man) city, car, happiness
    Proper nouns   David, Lake Charles, Mustang

Capitalization   Beginning of a sentence, I, proper nouns.

Month 2   Verbs

All	Review the definition of a noun.
	Memorize the definition of a verb below.
	Give your student examples of verbs.
	Have him give you examples.
	Work with your student to identify the verbs in the copywork model.
	Circle the nouns blue and the verbs red.
Younger students	You may choose to teach only action verbs.
Older students	Teach the different types of verbs: action, state of being, linking, and helping verbs.
	Memorize state of being verbs
	Memorize list of helping verbs

Verbs   <u>circle red</u>   a word that expresses action, state of being, or links two words together

    Action verbs   (jump) run, think, have, skip, throw, say, dance, smell
    State of being   any form of to be = **am, are, is, was, were, be, being, been**
    Linking verbs   **any state of being verb** and any verb that can logically be replaced by a "to be" verb
                          She **seems** nice. She is nice. The flower **smells** stinky. The flower is stinky.
    Helping verbs   am, are, is, was, were, be, being, been, do, does, did, has, have, had, may, might, must
                          shall, will, can, should, would, could

Month 3 *Pronouns*

All	Review the definitions of nouns and verbs.
	Memorize the definition of a pronoun below.
	Give your student examples of pronouns.
	Have him give you examples.
	Help your student to identify the pronouns in the copywork model.
	Circle the nouns blue, the verbs red, and the pronouns green.
All	Teach the four types of sentences.

Pronouns <u>circle green</u>   a word that replaces a noun in a sentence. It may take the place of a person, place, thing, or idea.

Jack ran.	(He) ran.
Ike hit Al and Mary.	Ike hit **them**
The car is very nice.	**That** is very nice.

Types of sentences and punctuation

Declarative or statement	I have a blue dress. The ground is wet from the rain.
Interrogative or question	Will we have dessert today? What time is it?
Imperative or demand	Come here. Sit down. Mop the floor at 2:00.
Exclamation	I sold my painting for ten million dollars!

Month 4 — Adjectives

All	Review the definitions of a noun, verb, and pronouns.
	Memorize the definition of an adjective below.
	Give your student examples of adjectives.
	Have him give you examples.
	Help your student to identify the adjectives in the copywork model.
	Circle the nouns blue, the verbs red, pronouns green, and the adjectives yellow.
All	Review the four types of sentences.
Older students	Learn about Attributive, Predicate, or Demonstrative Adjectives

Adjectives <u>circle yellow</u>   a word that describes a noun or a pronoun

(When studying adverbs, you may have your student draw an arrow to the word being modified.)

I want candy.	I want **five** candies.	
the car	the **red** car	Attributive adj. (adjective is before the noun)
I like shoes.	I like **those** shoes.	Demonstrative adj. (this, that, these, those)
The tall girl	The girl is **tall**.	Predicate adjectives (tall, stinky, angry)
The stinky dog	The dog smells **stinky**.	
The angry man	The man appeared **angry**.	

Possessives   words that show ownership

Mine, yours, his, hers, ours, theirs, whose	possessive pronouns (used alone)
My car, **your** house, **his** shirt, **her** computer	possessive pronouns
	(used with a noun and identified as an adjective in many grammar programs)
Jane's car, Mike's shoes, Jesus' parables,	singular possessive nouns
Mom and Dad's sons, my sisters' names, children's books	plural possessive nouns

Month 5 — Adverbs

All
Review the definitions of nouns, verbs, pronouns, adjectives
Memorize the definition of an adverb below.
Give your student examples of adverbs.
Have him give you examples.
Help your student to identify the adverbs in the copywork model.
Circle the nouns blue, the verbs red, pronouns green, adjectives yellow, and adverbs orange.

Older students
Learn about possessive pronouns and possessive nouns

Adverbs <u>circle orange</u>   a word that describes a verb, another adverb, or an adjective

Don't run.	Don't run **inside**.	**Modifies the verb** tells where
The man ran.	The man ran **swiftly**.	tells how
It will rain.	It will rain **soon**.	tells when
		Modifies adjectives or other adverbs
The dog is hairy.	The dog is **very** hairy.	tells extent (modifies hairy)

Month 6 — Prepositions

All
Review the definitions of nouns, verbs, pronouns, adjectives, adverbs
Memorize the definition of a preposition below.
Give your student examples of prepositions.
Have him give you examples.
Help your student to identify the prepositions in the copywork model.
Circle the nouns blue, the verbs red, pronouns green, adjectives yellow, adverbs orange, and prepositions purple.

Older students
Learn about prepositional phrases and commas
Underline the prepositional phrase in the model.
Memorize list of prepositions

Preposition <u>circle purple</u>   a word that shows relationship between one noun and another word in the sentence (Prepositional phrases are to be underlined)

He is **on** <u>the box</u>.   He is **under** <u>the box</u>.   He went **around** <u>the box</u>.   He is **in** <u>the box</u>.

Commas   3 items or more in a series
The elephant**,** the mouse**,** and the gnat are best friends.
I like red**,** green**,** and orange vegetables.

Common Prepositions
About, above, across, after, against along, among, around, at, before, behind, below, beneath, beside, between, beyond, by, down, during, except, for, from, in, inside, into, like, near, of, off, on, onto, out, over, past, since, through, throughout, to, toward, under, underneath, until, up, upon, with, within, without

Month 7 — Conjunctions

All
Review the definitions of nouns, verbs, pronouns, adjectives, adverbs, and prepositions
Memorize the definition of a conjunction below.
Give your student examples of conjunctions.
Have him give you examples.
Help your student to identify the conjunctions in the copywork model.
Circle the nouns blue, the verbs red, pronouns green, adjectives yellow, adverbs orange, prepositions purple, and the conjunctions brown.

Older students
Learn Quotations marks

Conjunction <u>circle brown</u>   a word that links words, phrases, or clauses **(and, but, or, nor, so, for, yet)**

Jamie **and** I left. **(words)**
The blue sky, the warm sun, **and** the rainbow of flowers brightened my spirits. **(phrases)**
He is tall, **for** both of his parents are tall.
  (independent clauses, must have a comma when combining main clauses)

Quotation Marks   Use quotation marks to set off direct quotations.

"No, I don't like peas**,**" answered the little boy.   beginning of a sentence
The little boy answered**,** "I don't like peas**.**"   end of a sentence
"No**,**" answered the little boy**,** "I don't like peas**.**"   middle of a sentence

Month 8 — Interjections

All
Review the definitions of nouns, verbs, pronouns, adjectives, adverbs, prepositions, and conjunctions
Memorize the definition of an interjection below.
Give your student examples of interjections.
Have him give you examples.
Help your student to identify the interjections in the copywork model.
Circle the nouns blue, the verbs red, pronouns green, adjectives yellow, adverbs orange, prepositions purple, conjunctions brown, and interjections black.

Older students   Learn semi-colon use

Interjection <u>circle black</u>   a word that expresses emotion, sometimes but not always, sudden or intense.

Yes! I want ice cream too! **Well**, we're late because the car broke down.

Semi-colons   replace commas and conjunctions when combining two independent clauses

My family is going to the farm**, and** we are going to have a grand time riding horses.
My family is going to the farm; we are going to have a grand time riding horses.

Models from Chapter I

Note: (Models taken from the beginning of a paragraph are indented as well as models from one line dialogue.)

from **The Cowherd Who Became a Poet, Caedmon**
from <u>Fifty Famous People</u>
   by James Baldwin

Out of doors the wind was blowing. The men heard it as it whistled through the trees.

   Then Caedmon had a strange dream. He thought that a wonderful light was shining around him.

from **The Caliph and the Poet**
from <u>Fifty Famous People</u>
   by James Baldwin

Al Mansur loved poetry and was fond of hearing poets repeat their own verses. Sometimes, he gave the poet a prize.

The caliph laughed outright, and so did every one that heard him. Then he ordered his treasurer to pay the poet five hundred pieces of gold.

from **A Lesson in Humility, Haroun-al-Raschid**
from <u>Fifty Famous People</u>
   by James Baldwin

All the noblest men of Persia and Arabia were there. Many wise men and poets and musicians had also been invited.

The caliph's eyes were filled with tears. Emotion choked him. He covered his face and wept.

from **The Sons of the Caliph**
from <u>Fifty Famous People</u>
   by James Baldwin

But they dared not quarrel and at last agreed that each should carry one shoe. Thus, the honor would be divided.

They did nothing that was beneath the dignity of princes. Indeed, they honored themselves by honoring you.

from **How a Prince Learned to Read**
from <u>Fifty Famous People</u>
   by James Baldwin

A thousand years ago, boys and girls did not learn to read. Books were very scarce and very precious.

A few weeks passed by. Then one morning, Alfred went into his mother's room with a smiling, joyous face.

from **King Alfred and the Cakes, Alfred the Great**
from <u>Fifty Famous Stories Retold</u>
   by James Baldwin

King Alfred was very willing to watch the cakes, but he had far greater things to think about.

In a little while, the woman came back. The cakes were smoking on the hearth. They were burned to a crisp. Ah, how angry she was!

from **King Alfred and the Beggar**
from <u>Fifty Famous Stories Retold</u>
   by James Baldwin

About noon, a ragged beggar came to the king's door and asked for food.

In the morning, the king arose early and crossed over to the mainland. Then he blew his horn three times very loudly.

from **King Canute on the Seashore**
from <u>Fifty Famous Stories Retold</u>
   by James Baldwin

The great men and officers who were around King Canute were always praising him.

The king was a man of sense. He grew very tired of hearing such foolish speeches.

from **The Sons of William the Conqueror**
from Fifty Famous Stories Retold
   by James Baldwin

There was once a great king of England who was called William the Conqueror. He had three sons.

The first who came into the room was Robert. He was a tall, willful lad and was nicknamed Short Stocking.

from **The White Ship**
from Fifty Famous Stories Retold
   by James Baldwin

One summer Prince William went with his father across the sea to look after their lands in France.

The sea was smooth. The winds were fair. And no one thought of danger.

from **The King and His Hawk**
from Fifty Famous Stories Retold
   by James Baldwin

The king rode slowly along. He had once seen a spring of clear water near this pathway. If he could only find it now!

The king stopped. He forgot his thirst. He thought only of the poor dead bird lying on the ground below him.

from **King John and the Abbot**
from Fifty Famous Stories Retold
   by James Baldwin

Lend me your servants, horse, and gown. I will go up to London and see the king.

"Indeed, indeed!" said the king, and he laughed to himself. "How long shall I live? Come, you must tell me to the very day."

from **The Shepherd Boy Painter**
from Fifty Famous People
   by James Baldwin

The stranger's name was Cimabue. He was the most famous painter of the time.

In the morning, when he looked at the picture, he saw a fly on the man's nose. He tried to brush it off, but it remained there.

from **The Hunted King, Robert I king of the Scots**
from Fifty Famous People
   by James Baldwin

Sometimes two or three faithful friends were with him. Sometimes he was alone. Sometimes his enemies were very close.

So she called her two sons. They were tall and strong young men, and they gladly promised to go with the king and help him.

from **The Black Douglas**
from Fifty Famous Stories Retold
   by James Baldwin

In the dusk, she could not make out what they were. And so she pointed them out to one of the watchmen.

The woman watched them until the last one had passed around a corner out of sight. She was not afraid.

from **The Story of William Tell**
from Fifty Famous Stories Retold
   by James Baldwin

One day this tyrant set up a tall pole in the public square and put his own cap on the top of it.

The arrow whistled through the air. It struck the apple fairly in the center and carried it away. The people who saw it shouted with joy.

from "TRY, TRY AGAIN!"
from Fifty Famous People
  by James Baldwin

Just as he spoke, the ant lost its footing and fell to the ground. But it still held on to the grain of wheat.

Tamerlane watched the brave little insect. It tried three times, four times, a dozen times, twenty times, but always with the same result.

from Arnold Winkelried
from Fifty Famous Stories Retold
  by James Baldwin

Some came with bows and arrows, some with scythes and pitchforks, and some with only sticks and clubs.

They snatched spears and shields from their foes. They had no thought of fear. They only thought of their homes and their dear native land.

from The Horseshoe Nails
from Fifty Famous People
  by James Baldwin

"Oh, well," said the groom, "won't six nails do? Put three in each shoe. King Richard will be impatient."

So he quickly finished the shoeing, and the groom hurried to lead the horse to the king.

from King Edward and his Bible
from Parker's Second Reader
  by Mrs. L.H. Sigourney.

One day he heard that one of his teachers was sick. Immediately, he retired to pray for him.

Edward the Sixth died when he was sixteen years old. He was beloved by all for his goodness and piety.

from **Sir Humphrey Gilbert**
from Fifty Famous Stories Retold
   by James Baldwin

When they were three days from land, the wind failed, and the ships lay floating on the waves.

Great white icebergs came drifting around them. In the morning, the little ships were almost lost among the floating mountains of ice.

from **Sir Walter Raleigh**
from Fifty Famous Stories
   by James Baldwin

He found two things in this country that the people of England knew very little about. One was the potato, and the other was tobacco.

He ran out for some water. He found a pail that was quite full. He hurried back and threw the water into Sir Walter's face.

from **Which Was the King?**
from Fifty Famous People
   by James Baldwin

On February 27, 1594, King Henry IV was finally crowned the King of France.

"No, sir," answered the boy. "I am looking for the king. They say he is hunting in the woods. So I'm waiting to see him."

from **Sir Philip Sidney**
from Fifty Famous Stories
   by James Baldwin

The air was hot and stifling. The sun shone down without pity on the wounded soldiers lying in the blood and dust.

What a brave, noble man he was! The name of Sir Philip Sidney will never be forgotten.

Models from Chapter II

from How Jack Went to Seek His Fortune
from English Fairy Tales
by Joseph Jacobs

So on they went, jiggelty jolt, jiggelty jolt. They went a little further, and they met a goat.

He hadn't gone very far before he met a cat. "Where are you going, Jack?" said the cat.

from Jack Hannaford
from English Fairy Tales
by Joseph Jacobs

It was not long that Jack waited after receiving the money. He went off as fast as he could walk.

There was no time to waste words. So the farmer mounted his horse and rode off after Jack Hannaford.

from Lazy Jack
from English Fairy Tales
by Joseph Jacobs

He would do nothing but bask in the sun in the summer and sit by the corner of the hearth in the winter. So they called him Lazy Jack.

On Wednesday, Jack went out again and hired himself to a cow keeper. The cow keeper gave him a jar of milk for his day's work.

from Little Red Riding Hood
from English Fairy Tales
by Flora Annie Steel

Then he shut the door, put on Grannie's nightcap, and rolled himself well up in the bed.

Little Red Riding Hood had been amusing herself by gathering nuts, running after butterflies, and picking flowers.

from **The Magpie's Nest**
from English Fairy Tales
   by Joseph Jacobs

Finally, the only bird that remained was the turtledove. But the turtledove hadn't paid any attention all along.

"Now I know all about it," said the blackbird, and off he flew. And that's how the blackbirds make their nests to this very day.

from **The Miller's Guest**
from A Child's World Reader
   by Hetty Browne, Sarah Withers, W.K. Tate

At last, he heard the sound of horse's hoofs. Someone was coming. Was it friend or foe?

"I'll keep your secret," said the hunter. "Don't fear. The king shall never know more than he knows now."

from **The Old Woman and Her Pig**
from English Fairy Tales
   by Joseph Jacobs

She said to the dog, "Dog! Bite pig! Piggy won't go over the stile, and I shall not get home tonight." But the dog wouldn't.

As soon as the cow had eaten the hay, she gave the old woman the milk. And away she went with it in a saucer to the cat.

from **Other Wise Men of Gotham**
from Fifty Famous Stories Retold
   by James Baldwin

So they went out with their axes. And soon all the roads and paths to the town were filled with logs and brush.

Everybody was in great fright. The men ran from house to house, carrying the news and asking one another what they should do.

from **Saddle to Rags**
from A Child's World Reader
   by Hetty Browne, Sarah Withers, W.K. Tate

The silly old man bridled old Tib and saddled her too. And away they started.

"Well, if you will have it, you can go for it," cried the old man. Then he threw his old saddlebags over a hedge.

from **The Shoemaker and the Elves**
from A Beacon Second Reader
   by James H. Fassett

The next morning he went into his shop to make the shoes. What did he see? A pair of shoes, all nicely made and ready to be sold.

They saw the little coats, the tiny stockings, and the neat little shoes. They clapped their hands for joy.

from **A Story of Robin Hood**
from Fifty Famous Stories Retold
   by James Baldwin

The next day Robin stood in the same place. He had not been there long when he saw the same young man coming down the road.

But he did not seem to be so happy this time. He had left his scarlet coat at home, and at every step, he sighed and groaned.

from **The Story of the Three Little Pigs**
   by Unknown

"Then I'll puff and I'll huff, and I'll blow your house in!" So he huffed and he puffed, and he puffed and he huffed.

Well, the little Pig got up at five and got the turnips and was home again before six.

from **Three Men of Gotham**
from Fifty Famous Stories Retold
   by James Baldwin

One day two men of Gotham met on a bridge. Hodge was coming from the market, and Peter was going to the market.

"Now look at me," he said, "and learn a lesson." And he opened the mouth of the sack and poured all the meal into the river.

from **Tom Thumb**
from The Beacon Second Reader
   by James H. Fassett.

Tom leaned over the edge of the bowl to see how it was made. He slipped, and in he went, head first.

Tom crawled out of the pudding, climbed out of the basket, and ran home. His mother washed him and put him to bed.

Models from Chapter III

from **Aladdin**
from <u>The Ontario Readers: Fourth Book</u>
by Lowell

I had not a friend or a toy,
But I had Aladdin's lamp;

But I'd give all my lamps of silver bright
For the one that is mine no more;

from **Baa, Baa, Black Sheep**
from <u>Ring O' Roses A Nursery Rhyme Picture Book</u>
by Anonymous

Baa, baa, Black Sheep,
  Have you any wool?
Yes, marry, have I,
  Three bags full.

One for my master,
  And one for my Dame,
And one for the little boy
  That lives in the lane!

from **Cock-A-Doodle-Doo**
from <u>Ring O' Roses A Nursery Rhyme Picture Book</u>
by Anonymous

Cock-a-doodle-doo!
What is my dame to do?
Till master finds his fiddling-stick,
She'll dance without her shoe.

Cock-a-doodle-doo!
Dame has lost her shoe;
Gone to bed and scratched her head,
And can't tell what to do.

from **Columbus**
by Joaquin Miller

Brave Admiral, say but one word;
   What shall we do when hope is gone?"

The words leaped as a leaping sword:
   "Sail on! Sail on! And on!"

from **Rex Arthurus**
from <u>The Classic Mother Goose</u>
by Jacob Bigelow

When King Arthur ruled the land,
He ruled it like a king:

The king and queen partook thereof,
And all the court beside;
And what they did not eat that night,
The queen next morning fried.

from **The Greenwood Tree**
from <u>The Ontario Readers: Fourth Book</u>
by Shakespeare

Under the greenwood tree
Who loves to lie with me,
And tune his merry note
Unto the sweet bird's throat,

Who doth ambition shun
And loves to live i' the sun;
Seeking the food he eats,
And pleased with what he gets,

from **Ingratitude**
from <u>Poems Every Child Should Know</u>
by William Shakespeare

Blow, blow, thou winter wind,
Thou are not so unkind
As man's ingratitude;

Thy tooth is not so keen
Because thou are not seen,
Although thy breath be rude.

from **I Saw a Ship A-Sailing**
from <u>The Real Mother Goose</u>
by Unknown

The sails were made of silk,
And the masts were made of gold.

The four and twenty sailors
That stood between the decks
Were four and twenty white mice,
With chains about their necks.

from **Saint Bernard's Hymn**
from <u>The Library Of The World's Best Literature, Ancient And Modern, Vol 4</u>
collected by Charles Dudley Warner

O hope of every contrite heart!
  O joy of all the meek!

Jesu! our only joy be thou,
  As thou our prize wilt be!
Jesu! be thou our glory now
  And through eternity!

from The Sermon of St. Francis
by Henry Wadsworth Longfellow

"O brother birds," St. Francis said,
"Ye come to me and ask for bread,
But not with bread alone to-day
Shall ye be fed and sent away.

With flutter of swift wings and songs
Together rose the feathered throngs,
And singing scattered far apart;
Deep peace was in St. Francis' heart.

from To Market To Market
from Ring O' Roses A Nursery Rhyme Picture Book
by Anonymous

To market, to market, to buy a fat Pig;
Home again, home again, dancing a jig.

To market, to market, to buy a fat Hog;
Home again, home again, jiggety-jog.

Models from Chapter IV

from **The Frog's Travels**
from <u>A Story Hour Reader</u>
by Ida Coe and Alice J. Christie

One of the frogs lived in a pond near Tokyo. And the other lived in a little stream near Kyoto.

"What a pity that we are not taller!" said the Kyoto frog.
"Why?" asked the Tokyo frog.

from **How Indian Corn Came into the World**
from <u>Good Stories for Great Holidays</u>
adapted by Henry R. Schoolcraft

So Wunzh returned to his lodge and fasted and slept. On the third day, he became weak and faint.

He then returned to his father's lodge and partook sparingly of food. There he abode for some time.

from **The Necklace of Truth**
from <u>The Book of Stories for The Story-Teller</u>
by Jean Mace

"I was ill for a long time," replied Coralie. "When I got well, mamma and papa gave me the necklace."

Poor Coralie did not wish to speak. The stones, however, began to dance up and down and to make a terrible clatter.

from **The Pancake**
from <u>East O' the Sun and West O' the Moon</u>
by Gudrun Thorne-Thomsen

So when it had rolled awhile it met a man.
"Good-day, pancake," said the man.

"Pancake, dear, don't roll so fast. Bide a bit and let me eat you up," said the hen.

from **Tale of a Dumb Witness**
from A Child's World Reader
   by Hetty Browne, Sarah Withers, W.K. Tate

Finding a tree with low branches, he tied his horse to one of them. Then he sat down to eat his dinner.

"See what your horse has done!" cried the rich man in an angry voice. "But you shall pay for it! You shall pay for it!"

from **The Three Billy Goats Gruff**
from East O' the Sun and West O' the Moon
   by Gudrun Thorne-Thomsen

First of all came the youngest Billy Goat Gruff to cross the bridge. "Trip, trap; trip, trap!" went the bridge.

"Trip, trap! Trip, trap!" went the bridge. For the Billy Goat was so heavy that the bridge creaked and groaned under him.

from **Why the Bear's Tail Is Short**
from A Beacon Second Reader
   by James H. Fassett

He threw off some of the best fish until he had enough for his dinner. Then Mr. Fox jumped from the wagon and began to eat the fish.

Mr. Fox ran away laughing and laughing at the trick he had played upon Mr. Bear.

from **The Wolf and the Seven Young Kids**
from A Beacon Reader
   by William and Jacob Grimm

When the little kids saw that it was white, they thought this was really their mother. They opened the door.

When at last the wicked wolf did wake up, the great stones inside him made him feel very heavy. He was thirsty, too.

Made in the USA
San Bernardino, CA
24 March 2016